REMBRANDT
SELECTED DRAWINGS
BY
OTTO BENESCH

REMBRANDT

SELECTED DRAWINGS

BY

OTTO BENESCH

MCMXLVII

LONDON : PHAIDON PRESS LTD

NEW YORK : OXFORD UNIVERSITY PRESS

MADE IN GREAT BRITAIN

1947

PRINTED IN ENGLAND AT THE CURWEN PRESS

ACKNOWLEDGEMENT

I HAVE to thank particularly the following private collectors who have generously helped in the provision of photographs and have permitted the reproduction of their drawings:
Mr. Oscar Bondi; Sir Herbert Bonn, London; Dr. A. Bredius, The Hague; Mr. J. de Bruijn, Spiez; Mr. Louis C. G. Clarke, Cambridge; Dr. Tobias Christ, Basel; Mr. Atherton Curtis, Paris; His Grace the Duke of Devonshire, Chatsworth; Dr. G. Falck, Copenhagen; Captain G. M. Gathorne-Hardy, Newbury, Berkshire; M. Lucien Guiraud, Paris; Mr. O. Gutekunst, London; Mr. Robert von Hirsch, Basel; Mr. V. Koch, London; Mr. S. Kramarsky, New York City; His Highness the Prince of Liechtenstein, Vienna; Mr. F. Lugt, The Hague; Lady Melchett, London; Captain H. S. Reitlinger, London; Dr. A. Hamilton Rice, New York City; Mr. Lessing J. Rosenwald, Jenkintown, Pa.; Dr. Paul J. Sachs, Cambridge, Massachusetts; Dr. Charles Simon, Zürich; Baroness Six, Amsterdam; Mr. A. Stroelin, Lausanne; Mr. L. H. Walters, London; Dr. A. Welcker, Amsterdam.

O.B.

CONTENTS

INTRODUCTION

REMBRANDT'S ART OF DRAWING
IN THE JUDGEMENT
OF HIS CONTEMPORARIES

MODERN criticism has so often considered Rembrandt as a unique figure rising above and beyond his surroundings and his time that his significance as a representative of his era has been underestimated. In admiring him for his struggle against the prevailing taste of his age, some critics[1] fail to make clear how well he represents and sums up the artistic endeavour of his century. This applies particularly to Rembrandt's activity as a draughtsman. Of the three greatest draughtsmen of the seventeenth century, Rubens, Callot, and Rembrandt, Rembrandt was, beyond any doubt, the most representative. The judgement of his contemporaries, divided and inconsistent as it was in regard to his paintings, was unanimous and unrestrained in praise of his art of drawing.

It is evident from literary documents that Rembrandt's idea of drawing as an instantaneous reaction to visual inspiration or impulsive expression of inner vision seemed something new and stupendous to his contemporaries. Rembrandt devoted especial attention to drawing, not only as an artist and teacher, but also as a collector. The first documents which report about Rembrandt's activity as a purchaser at public sales[2] prove his prevailing interest in drawings and prints. The inventory of his property taken on 25 and 26 July 1656[3] is surprising because of the wealth of prints and drawings in his art collection. The collection was so rich that a special sale had to be arranged in the Autumn of 1658 for the 'Papier Kunst' (paper art), consisting of 'works of art of various of the most outstanding Italian, French, German, and Netherlandish masters, collected by the afore-mentioned Rembrandt van Rijn with great amateurship'.[4]

Just as those works of other masters were new experiences and sources of inspiration to him, so his own drawings became in time objects of admiring emulation to his pupils and to connoisseurs of art. His pupil Govaert Flink gathered an important collection of Rembrandt drawings, mainly landscapes, which later entered the collection of His Grace the Duke of Devonshire. His wealthy friend, the sea

[1] For example, Carl Neumann in his famous biography of the master.

[2] C. Hofstede de Groot, Die Urkunden über Rembrandt, Quellenstudien zur holländischen Kunstgeschichte III, Haag, 1906, No. 51: 9 March 1637. ib. No. 56: 9 February 1638.

[3] ib. No. 169.　[4] ib. No. 197.

painter Jan van Capelle, had about five hundred drawings by Rembrandt in his extensive drawing collection: historical representations, genre studies, and landscapes.[1] Members of the Guild of St. Luke in Leiden, who were art collectors, sold and bought drawings by the master in 1645.[2]

In the second half of the seventeenth century, the number of references to Rembrandt drawings in inventories of art collections in Amsterdam increases. A Rembrandt drawing finds particular mention in the inventory of the collector Dirck Thomas Molengraeff in 1654.[3] Jan Boursse, the brother of the painter of interiors, Esaias Boursse, owned two large 'art books' filled with drawings and etchings by Rembrandt.[4]

The new estimation of the drawn sketch as a mode of artistic expression in its own right, which begins with Rembrandt, can be noticed in the historical and theoretical writings of his biographers and pupils. It is revealing to see how the growth of academic Classicism in the second half of the century could not prevent the theoreticians from giving praise and acknowledgement to Rembrandt's personal and vigorous manner, even if it violated their principles. Involuntarily, the admiration for Rembrandt's greatness as a draughtsman breaks through, although more or less tempered by criticism. This fact proves how much the draughtsman Rembrandt realized the artistic striving of the seventeenth century.

The earliest foreigner to give a literary report on Rembrandt was the German, Joachim von Sandrart, who wrote about him in his 'Teutsche Academie der edlen Bau-, Bild-, und Mahlerey-Kuenste', published in Nuremberg and Francfort in 1675–1679. Sandrart had lived in Amsterdam in the years 1637–1642, and there became acquainted with the 'Baroque' Rembrandt, but not with the later development of the master, with the 'Classical' Rembrandt. Sandrart, about the time of the publication of his book, had already become an exponent of the fashionable classicistic tendency of the time. He, therefore, criticized the heavy Baroque style of the Rembrandt of the early Amsterdam period, which by then had been discarded as old-fashioned. He emphasizes Rembrandt's adherence to nature and native tradition, and his opposition to the rules of anatomy and perspective, and to the use of ancient statues and Raphael's art of drawing. We know that this statement is inaccurate. The inventory of Rembrandt's art collection testifies to the contrary, but, of course, those factors gained highest importance for Rembrandt in his mature and late periods, which were lesser known to Sandrart. Nevertheless, Sandrart was too much of a man of the Baroque century not to recognize Rembrandt's great importance for a specifically Baroque notion of drawing. He writes: '. . . considering the demands

---

[1] ib. No. 350. See also our No. 61.   [2] ib. No. 103.   [3] ib. No. 153.

[4] ib. No. 322. It was the habit in former centuries to keep prints and drawings unmounted, inserted loosely between leaves of fine paper which were fastened into stiff leather covers.

of a work, he approved of light and shadow, and of the outlines of all things, even if they were against the rules of perspective provided they were well-done according to his opinion and served the purpose. Furthermore, as neat outlines have to appear correctly in their place, he avoided all danger by filling in dark shadows with the sole purpose of keeping together the universal harmony. . . .' This is quite a clever characterization of Rembrandt's mode of drawing in the late 1630s, although given from a point of view opposed to him.

The most intelligent praise which a foreigner gave to Rembrandt was, significantly enough, that of a representative of the æsthetics of the Italian High Baroque. Filippo Baldinucci wrote about Rembrandt in his 'Comminciamento e progresso dell'arte dell'intagliare in rame, colle vite di molti dei più eccellenti Maestri della stessa Professione' (Florence 1686). He reports on the appreciation of Rembrandt's drawings and quotes the Danish Rembrandt pupil Bernhard Keihl, who had told him that, at a public sale, one of Rembrandt's drawings which showed little, almost nothing, attained a price of thirty scudi.

In Roger de Piles' 'Abregé de la Vie des Peintres' (Paris 1699) the classicistic predisposition becomes still more evident than in Sandrart's book. France by now had obtained the undisputed leadership in the classicistic taste. Hence it is altogether natural that De Piles meets Rembrandt's paintings with a criticism like Sandrart's, and perhaps not entirely independent of him: '. . . on ne verra point dans Rembrandt, ni le Goût de Raphael, ni celuy de l'Antique, ni pensées Poétiques, ni élégance de Dessein; on y trouvera seulement, tout ce que le Naturel de son Pais, conçû par une vive imagination, est capable de produire. . . .' 'C'est la raison pour laquelle Rembrandt n'a pas beaucoup peint de sujets d'Histoires, quoy qu'il ait dessiné une infinité de pensées qui n'ont pas moins de sel et de piquant que les productions des meilleurs Peintres. Le grand nombre de ses Desseins que j'ay entre mes mains en est une preuve convaincante à qui voudra leur rendre justice.'

All the limitations of classicistic æsthetics could not keep De Piles from paying just tribute to Rembrandt's eminent art of drawing. He even recognizes correctly how many of Rembrandt's ideas entered his drawings only, which represent a category of work in its own right, equal if not superior to the greatest creations of painting.

Under the influence of the critics of the late seventeenth century Classicism stands the judgement of Rembrandt's fellow-countryman Arnold Houbraken, given in his 'Groote Schouburgh der Nederlantsche konstschilders en schilderessen' (Amsterdam 1718–1721). Also here, in spite of the narrowness of the judgement of Rembrandt's paintings, we meet with an intelligent appraisal of Rembrandt's drawings: 'With regard to art, he was prolific in ideas, hence quite frequently there can be seen a large number of different studies of one and the same subject, full of variations with regard to character, attitudes and arrangement of garments . . .' ' . . . of his art of etching, several hundred works are known among the print lovers, and no less a number of pen sketches on paper in which the emotions of the soul caused by different events are shown so artistically and clearly in their essential features that it is a marvel to look at. Anger, hatred, grief, joy, and so on, everything is delineated so naturally that one can read in the penstrokes what each one wants to say.'

In spite of the fluctuation of judgement on Rembrandt's pictorial creations, there seems to have been a continuous tradition for appreciating his drawings, however adverse ruling taste and fashion may have been in times to the greatness and uniqueness of the master.

REMBRANDT'S METHOD AND TECHNIQUE
OF DRAWING

THE best informants on Rembrandt's method and technique of drawing are the drawings themselves. The practice of drawing was for Rembrandt a continuous one, underlying his entire artistic study and activity. We reach this conclusion because of the unusual number of drawings still preserved after so many losses. We have to assume that the restless activity of the young Rembrandt, of which Constantijn Huyghens wrote in his autobiography,[1] consisted largely of drawing, although the number of drawings preserved from his Leiden years, when Rembrandt was still a beginner, is relatively small. Even at dusk, the working hours of the draughtsman were not over. They continued by lamp- or candle-light in the circle of his studio or his family. (We see this represented in the etchings Hind 191 and 231; our Nos. 5 and 7 show some of the results.)[2] For the sharply confined streams of light in which the young Rembrandt represented his models, it was more or less irrelevant whether they came from a natural or an artificial source, provided that the light showed the model in the intended relief. Drawing in these early years concerned chiefly models at rest. Later, the problems of movement gained greater importance.

The nature of Rembrandt's subjects as much as the mode of their representation rarely induced the master to use the large folio sheets which were favoured by the Italian and Flemish Baroque masters. We find them occasionally used for a portrait commission (No. 43), for a profane or religious representation which the artist wished to expand in a cartoonlike manner (Nos. 4 and 44), for copies after other masters (No. 45), and only very exceptionally for a study from nature. Half- and

[1] Hofstede de Groot, Urkunden. No. 18.
[2] O. Benesch, An Early Group Portrait Drawing by Rembrandt, *The Art Quarterly*, Winter 1940.

REMBRANDT'S TECHNIQUE OF DRAWING

quarter-sheets were his most favoured sizes, but he frequently confined himself to even smaller pieces of paper, and this not only for hasty annotations, but even for carefully considered compositional drawings for large canvasses, especially in his later years, when he did not hesitate to use the scrap nearest at hand (Nos. 274 and 279). If during his work the size turned out to be not large enough, Rembrandt enlarged the surface by adding a piece of paper to the main sheet.

Rembrandt seems to have used the paper in two forms, either fastened to a pad or to a drawing-board, or bound into a sketch-book. The latter he apparently favoured for out-of-door sketching, especially of landscapes. The contents of some of those sketchbooks can be reconstructed from their measurements (see No. 178). Both forms were in use in Rembrandt's workshop, as we may deduce from two drawings by pupils of Rembrandt's, representing the master among his disciples drawing after a model in the nude, one in Weimar,[1] the other in Darmstadt.[2] Even the old Netherlandish mode of drawing on prepared paper with the silver-point in a little sketchbook has been once or twice attempted by Rembrandt, and then discontinued.

The working before the model was a very methodical one. This is proved not only by the two mentioned representations of Rembrandt's drawing class, but also by the results of these studies (see Nos. 148, 149, 242, 243). As Rembrandt himself used to draw amid his pupils, groups of drawings occasionally show one and the same model in the same pose, seen from different angles—an admonition to distinguish carefully between master's and pupil's work.[3] The model was placed in effective light, usually by closed lower shutters of the opposite windows (see No. 244).

Out-of-door drawing demanded quite a different approach. There, everything depended on the quick grasp of a figure group or a single motive, on the rapid apperception of the essential elements in features, postures, and expressions. Many street scenes and sheets of studies are the results. Or the task was the deepening into a landscape motive resting in the quiet spatial grandeur of the Dutch country. The simple pen or black chalk replaced the more elaborate and mixed technical procedures which occur only in indoor drawings.

Rembrandt used almost exclusively grainy white paper (sometimes of a yellowish or brownish shade) as a drawing surface. In a few cases, he tinged the paper with a greyish or brownish hue before he began to draw. Occasionally, he enjoyed the soft silky lustre of Japanese paper, which he employed also for early impressions of his etchings. He used this paper when he intended to give his drawings a precious exotic flavour, e.g. his copies after Indian miniatures (Nos. 229–232).

[1] Prestel Gesellschaft II, 25.
[2] Jahrbuch der Preussischen Kunstsammlungen 45 (1924), p. 197.
[3] C. Hofstede de Groot, Rembrandt's onderwijs aan zijne leerlingen. Bredius Feest-Bundel, The Hague. 1915.

However, infinite as the varieties of the artistic effects of Rembrandt's drawings are, his tools and media were relatively simple. The drawings fall technically into two main groups: the group of chalk drawings and the group of bistre and ink drawings. The latter is by far the larger one, as the medium was most akin to Rembrandt's genius. The chalk used by Rembrandt was mostly red and black chalk. In rare cases, yellow crayon and white chalk occur, the former as an additional colour touch (No. 88), the latter for applying highlights. In his youth, Rembrandt seems to have started with chalk drawing. This medium prevails in importance over bistre during the Leiden years; the realistic studies of old men glow in its fiery red. The soft touch with which Rembrandt applies the black chalk often lends to the drawings a wonderful silvery hue, porous and soaked with light. Sometimes, red and black chalk are combined (No. 3); then, the veiny diaphanous flesh parts gleam in red. The exclusive use of red chalk in a drawing was discarded by Rembrandt after 1640. He kept black chalk until the beginning of the 1650s, and favoured it especially for landscape sketches.

In drawings of a very elaborate pictorial effect (Nos. 43, 44, 87, 88, 94, 148), Rembrandt used chalks combined with pen- and brush-work in bistre, Indian ink, white body-colour, and sometimes even oil colour. Yet these drawings are exceptions.

Black lead was very seldom employed by Rembrandt. Where it occurs in addition to black chalk it raises the suspicion that it may have been added by another hand.

Rembrandt's liquid media consisted of bistre, ink, Indian ink, and white body-colour.[1] He applied them with a quill-pen, a reed-pen, and a brush. The flexible quill-pen with its rapid or considerate loops and curves was most appropriate to the style of the early, the 'Baroque' Rembrandt. The reed-pen with its brittle character suggests itself for straight lines, either sharp ones, if drawn along the edge, or broad ones, if drawn along the shaft. Therefore Rembrandt favoured this instrument most in his later years, as it is appropriate to the firm tectonic character of his mature art. The reed has the quality of absorbing the medium. The half-dry pen yields strokes of a fluid iridescence, of a peculiar vibrancy which is most expressive of the magic transparency of the art of the mature Rembrandt. Some of the late drawings equal the paintings in immaterial fluorescence (No. 264).

It would be incorrect to assume that the use of these instruments has chronological limitations. Rembrandt used the reed-pen occasionally already in the 1630s, although in combination with the quill (Nos. 77, 78). On the other hand, we find the use of quill-pen down to the late years (No. 280, HdG 1416, and all the copies after Indian miniatures).

The brush was used for filling in the washes between the pen lines and also as a proper instrument of drawing. Rembrandt liked, especially in his mature drawings,

[1]The best analysis of drawing media is to be found in Joseph Meder, Die Handzeichnung, Wien 1923.

to wash with the brush dipped in water over the linework, thus achieving a most admirable blending of the forms in the atmosphere. The most delicate hues, which Rembrandt spread over the linework of his mature landscape drawings, were achieved by dilution of the medium in water. The importance of the brush as a drawing instrument increased of course in the later time (see No. 249), yet it appears also in the earliest years (HdG 682). We often see in Rembrandt's drawings, especially mere pen-drawings, a kind of subtle, dry shadow which gently touches the surface of the paper, leaving uncovered the deepenings of the grain, and does not fill it completely like washed shadows. This kind of shadow was applied with the finger tip, rubbing slightly a part of the drawing as long as it was in a wet condition. It has a particularly suggestive atmospheric effect.

It is amazing what variety of colour expression Rembrandt achieved in his monochrome media, almost as much as in his paintings. Bistre was his most favoured medium. We find it in all shades and grades, from deep sonorous brown to light saffron-yellow. We find it in all transitions towards grey, often mixed with Indian ink. Indian ink was rarely used by Rembrandt as the only medium, but mostly in combination with bistre, especially when layers of washes had to be applied (No. 37). Rembrandt knew how to use the contrast of bistre and Indian ink for introducing warm and cool colour contrasts. The deep blackish brown of gall-nut ink occurs mainly in the early 1630s (Nos. 34–36). This medium tends to spread on the paper as on a blotter and finally to bite it through. Rembrandt, therefore, seems to have refrained from its use in later years, but he mixed ink frequently with bistre.

White body-colour was used by Rembrandt mainly for blotching out unsatisfactory parts in a drawing. Yet he applied it also for highlights or for tempering a shadow and turning it into a delicious silvery grey. If a larger part of the drawing had to be corrected, Rembrandt employed the method of superimposing a piece of paper.

We have a literary source informing us of the importance which Rembrandt attached to the practice, method, and media of drawing. His pupil Samuel van Hoogstraten wrote a theoretical book 'Inleyding tot de Hooge Schoole der Schilderkonst' (Rotterdam 1678), which is largely based on the instruction the author had received in the studio of Rembrandt. Hoogstraten stayed most of the years 1640–1648 with Rembrandt. The first book (Chapters 5–8) contains a treatise on drawing which is in large parts easily recognizable as a theoretical reflection of demonstration and oral advice in Rembrandt's studio. We there find confirmation of those facts on Rembrandt's method and technique of drawing which we learn from the drawings themselves.

Hoogstraten informs us that it is good fortune to have good drawings as models to draw from in one's early youth, because the student thus finds in a short time what others have to look for quite a while. The practice of copying the master's drawings was habitual in Rembrandt's studio during all the years. The disciples followed the models often rather closely, even in animated loops and curves, a fact which made the distinction to many eyes somewhat difficult. The case where both original and pupil's copy are preserved is very instructive for the critical understanding. Even nowadays, it sometimes happens that a good drawing is found to be a copy because the original emerges from oblivion.

Hoogstraten recommends to the art student the apperception of the essentials and their representation in a sketchy, generalizing way. The rough sketching is the first foundation of drawing, and is of such importance that one often achieves more through it than one can carry through with great labour afterwards. Hoogstraten even recommends the method of looking at the model with half-closed eyes in order to omit distracting details, and to indicate with loose strokes and touches the hollow shadows of eyes, nose, and mouth. Who would not think at these words of Rembrandt's magnificent brush drawings like No. 249? 'One can often express the character of the objects so strikingly by sketching that even most elaborate works can not compete. . . . So wonderfully potent are the sketches of great masters, and it is therefore all the more necessary to consider well the sketching.'

The author continues by advising the student how to proceed after the first traits have been secured. 'Give the outlines their proper swing, not in one pull which runs like a black wire around the form, but indicate them piece by piece with a light hand.' This is according to Rembrandt's principle of the silhouette opened by light and atmosphere, of the intermittent, breathing outline. The object represented is surrounded by space full of light and atmosphere; therefore, one has to observe the shadows from the very beginning, and to place them in the most effective way. 'Do not worry about the unevenness of a shadow . . . the effect will be more powerful, if you place the drawing at some distance.' Yet Hoogstraten warns of too quick and hasty a proceeding. We know from reports that Rembrandt was a slow and pondering worker, in spite of the apparent 'sketchiness' of many of his creations.

One of Rembrandt's most stupendous achievements was his ability to make the uncovered surface of the paper shine forth as if it were a source of light. The effect is the result of the harmonization of the shadows. We can observe this quality particularly well in Rembrandt's landscape drawings. Hoogstraten writes: 'Be parsimonious with all too intense lights, and let the ground of the paper work as much as possible.'

In the sixth chapter, Hoogstraten gives an illuminating account of tools and media, a verbal explanation of what we see in Rembrandt's drawings. We there learn about the practice of washing with red chalk dissolved in liquid, of blending of bistre and Indian ink. The combination of pen- and brush-drawing with touches of red and black chalk is praised as a method of achieving painterly effects. In his own simple drawings, Hoogstraten preserved many of those principles enunciated and practised by his master. He clung to them carefully in spite of the academic classicistic tenor of his book.

THE TYPES OF DRAWINGS

REMBRANDT kept large quantities of his drawings in his studio. They were arranged in portfolios for the practical needs of an artist who used his drawings as a repository of material for his works, and arranged according to subject-matter. Historical representations, genre scenes, figure studies, animals, landscapes formed the various groups.

This chapter deals with another arrangement of groups among the vast material, less obvious and primitive than the distinction of subject-matter: the differentiation of types according to the artistic purpose and meaning.

The distinction of types of drawings with regard to their purpose is easy in the case of artists before Rembrandt, particularly the Italians.[1] A clear and rational organization of the artistic process makes it quite evident what is a first idea, a sketch, a study after a model to be used in a composition, a complete project, a 'modello' for the patron, a cartoon, a study from nature, or a drawing in its own right. The position which drawing takes in the creative thinking and working of Rembrandt is so different that the boundaries fluctuate and the traditional distinctions lose their validity.

We may divide the drawings by Rembrandt first into two main categories: those done after nature, and those done from imagination. The study of nature meant something different to Rembrandt than to his forerunners. We know that he constantly recommended it to his pupils as the very basis of artistic creation. His approach was not the scientific one of the Italians. Neither was it the curiosity and eagerness of discovering nature which distinguished the Northern artists of the sixteenth century. His activity of studying nature consisted not merely in sharp observation, but he let himself be imbued with nature, and he thought and felt in terms of the real and natural only. It is a closer identification with nature than any other artist before him ever achieved. This relation to nature determined also Rembrandt's imagination. Even the most sacred and mysterious events were represented by him as happenings between human beings, endowed with body and soul.

[1] See Charles de Tolnay, History and Technique of Old Master Drawings, New York, 1943, Chapter III.

He glorified, transubstantiated them by the magic of light, but also this magic contained no spell which one could not experience by opening one's eye to the miracles of nature. This quality enabled Rembrandt to vivify all the abstractions of Mannerism. Never before have imaginations of an artist been so real as though they were studies from nature. It may, in fact, be the case that a religious subject was drawn as a study from nature (No. 64; HdG 987). The boundaries even between those two large categories of drawings fluctuate.

It is still more difficult to define the more specific types of drawings with regard to their purpose. To identify drawings as ends in themselves is not difficult in some elaborate and pretentious cases as the portrait No. 43 and the landscape No. 134. These were drawings for the patron or collector like portrait drawings by Hendrick Goltzius or landscape drawings by Albrecht Altdorfer.

In all copies after works of other masters Rembrandt had nothing more in mind than noting down for himself a work which evoked his interest. These copies may vary from large carefully-drawn folio sheets (Nos. 45, 82) to hasty pen sketches. Sometimes, the deviation from the model is so strong (No. 289) that Rembrandt's intention to recast the foreign work and to transform it completely into his own becomes most evident. This recasting may be an end in itself, yet may also lead on to a further work as in the case of No. 231, even if the drawing itself does not reveal such an intention.

This brings us to the difficult problem of determining in the case of Rembrandt what is a preparatory drawing. In the traditional sense, a preparatory drawing is either a project for a composition or a study after nature made for the purpose of realizing a composition.[1] The number of drawings which represent these types is relatively small in Rembrandt's case, although their number has considerably increased through research results of the last decades. The Nos. 2, 6, 13, 15, 30, 49, 50, 97, 104, 119, 137, 146, 147, 182, 193, 201, 211, 212, 252, 263, 279, are evidently com-positional projects, some of them for well-known works. Most of those sketches served as a suggestion for the artist himself, yet some of them (Nos. 146, 252, 279) may have also been shown to the patrons in order to give a rough idea what the completed work would be like. Rembrandt developed a particular style of geometrical abstraction which he favoured especially for such compositional projects, although it became a general feature of his figure drawings since the middle of the 1650s.

A careful 'modello', such as the Italians made, cannot be expected from Rembrandt. The most detailed preparatory drawing of which we know, the Anslo portrait No. 111, was used for immediate transfer to the copper plate. Yet we can hardly assume that Rembrandt always did such elaborate drawings for his portrait commissions; those for Jan Six' etching, for instance, are much more cursory

[1] In the case of a portrait both may coincide.

(No. 147, Val. 733). In the particular case of the Anslo, it may have meant a courtly convenience for the patron.

Studies from nature drawn for the purpose of realizing a composition to be painted or etched, are Nos. 3, 91, 98, 105, 106. This type of drawing, which had such an importance for the Italian artists and for the Northern Italianates like Rubens, is indeed rare with Rembrandt, a proof that he liked to follow a general line in executing a painting or etching, but preferred to have complete freedom in realizing the details, in the same way as Michelangelo did not keep strictly to clay models as other sculptors did, when he worked in stone.

The relation of a study from nature to a painting or etching is something special in the case of Rembrandt. He mostly studied and drew for the sake of studying and drawing, with no other aim in mind than obtaining the mastery of form and expression which can be achieved in that way. The mere study from nature becomes an end in itself. Northern artists like Duerer, Bruegel, De Gheyn had prepared the way for this notion of study from nature, but Rembrandt raised it to a much more comprehensive domain of artistic creation in its own right, notwithstanding the rhapsodic character of many of his studies. Out of this material of self-sufficient studies from nature, the inspiration for a painting or etching may grow. The studies of old men and beggars which Rembrandt drew with red and black chalk in his Leiden years are with few exceptions ends in themselves. Yet the deep impression which the humble figure of an old man, sketched in rapid strokes, made on Rembrandt gave rise to the vigorous etching 'St. Peter healing the Paralysed at the Gate of the Temple' (Hind 5). There, the drawing contained the spark out of which the flame grew. In the case of Nos. 16 and 19, Rembrandt used an existing study for an etching or painting without giving it a religious meaning. A drawing which is a lay-out for an etching from its beginning looks different (No. 12). It even happened that Rembrandt drew a figure which he made pose in the attitude of an already existing painting (No. 26). There we have the paradox case that a picture 'ends' in a drawing.

This was only possible with an artist like Rembrandt, whose creative phantasy flowed over with ideas, who never abandoned a thread once taken up, who continuously developed his inventions; an artist to whom the single work of art was not a foregone conclusion, but a living force which continued to work. It is evident that this state of affairs established a new relation between drawing and 'completed' work, before unknown in the history of art.

How an observation of reality, quickly noted down by Rembrandt with the pen, could develop in different ways we may see in No. 57. There, the group of the child with the dog prepares for the etching 'The Pancake Woman' (Hind 141). Yet Rembrandt added the group of the Prophet and the widow of Zarephath from his imagination, turning the impression into a biblical invention while a drawing of the genre subject itself (No. 56), done about the same time, is not at all a preparation of the etching in the proper sense.

The study of a cottage with a draw-well (No. 36) was chosen by Rembrandt among his drawings as suitable for the setting for the Parable of the Good Samaritan, which he had in mind to etch (Hind 101).

A domestic scene of an obstinate boy carried away by his mother from playmates, observed by Rembrandt in the fraction of a second, contained the germ which grew out to a large-sized mythological painting: Ganymede raped by the Eagle of Zeus (Bredius 471).

Rembrandt's landscape etchings, which make the impression of careful rendering of a bit of nature, are mostly free compositions built up from different motives which he had noted down in drawings (see Nos. 154, 170, 177, 179). He made use of his animal studies, sooner or later, in an etching or painting, although he did not have this in mind necessarily from the beginning (Nos. 35, 117, 183).

As numerous as the studies from nature are the drawings from imagination in Rembrandt's œuvre. We have discussed already the intentional projects for compositions. They are by far out-numbered by those drawings which are the result of Rembrandt's continuously productive phantasy. His artistic ideas and conceptions were in a state of constant evolution and development, changing indefatigably and procreating new forms, new solutions. They were given expression first of all in drawings. Hence the key position which drawing holds in Rembrandt's work.

Rembrandt was one of the greatest narrators of all times. Religious and profane history and the events of the daily life pass through his work as one unending stream of human life. This he interpreted most vividly in his drawings. The stories of the Bible—the only book which he read over and over again, which he illustrated with greater plasticity than anybody before or after him—were represented by him with such a nearness to life as if he had seen them with his own eyes. Life itself was something sacred to Rembrandt, independent of its religious or profane content. Life was to him first of all life of the soul, eloquence and expressiveness of the inner man. When a modest scene of the everyday life impressed his mind, and he recorded it in a drawing (No. 206), the step to the conjuring up of a Bible scene from a similar experience of life was not too far removed (Nos. 139, 140).

We need not assume that *every* genre scene was sketched immediately before the object. Even sheets of studies are sometimes proofs of Rembrandt's imaginative power (Nos. 92, 93). In this case, we may call them variations on a theme of expression.

In a broader sense, more or less all narrative drawings by Rembrandt share this quality. They were so to speak soliloquies of the master. This determines the unique relation of Rembrandt's drawings to his etched and printed œuvre. There are such relations, without detriment to the fact that the vast majority of the drawings are ends in themselves. They are, however, often relations which cannot be described in terms of 'preparatory drawing' or 'final result'. Ideas continued to work in Rembrandt's mind. The 'Hundred Guilder Print' (Nos. 104, 130) passed through different stages before it found its final version. The painting 'Manoah's Offering' of 1641 (Bredius 509) shows almost no similarity to the drawing No. 110, done a few years earlier. In the following decade, Rembrandt tried out several recastings of the composition (see Nos. 211, 212), together with entirely new versions (No. 233). The idea of the Last Supper of the Berlin drawing (No. 46), based on Leonardo da Vinci, re-echoes in 'Samson's Wedding' of 1638 (Bredius 507), and even in the 'Julius Civilis' of 1661 (Bredius 482). The great current of life, which forms the very content of Rembrandt's narrative art, seems to have imparted something of its nature, ever changing and nevertheless persevering, to the master's artistic concepts.

A special type of drawings is formed by the works of pupils which were corrected by the master (No. 188). Most of the preserved specimens date from the 1650s and show historical compositions which Rembrandt reworked with broad, effective strokes of the reed-pen. The corrections concern composition as well as gesture and expression.

CHRONOLOGY AND DEVELOPMENT

REMBRANDT research has already reached a point where an exact chronology of the drawings can be attempted. Very few drawings were dated by the master himself. Some can be exactly dated because they served as preparatory drawings for etchings or paintings. Still others can be dated approximately on the basis of artistic relations to other dated works. In this way, we are able to produce a documented specimen for almost every year or at least every other year from 1626 to 1662.

This basic stock of drawings, supplemented by similarities of structure and technical expression in dated etchings and paintings, permits us to arrange the material of Rembrandt's drawings in the order of a natural and organic development. Of course, the possibility of error has always to be considered: uncertainties and puzzles will probably always occur. Yet their number can be increasingly reduced. The research of recent years has brought growing clarity, and very grave errors can now be avoided.

The sources which contributed to the formation of Rembrandt's early style become clearly visible in the drawings of the Leiden years. Two main trends can be distinguished: the realistic Caravaggesque one, which was imparted to Rembrandt mainly by his master Pieter Lastman and Jan Pynas, but also through the painters of Utrecht, who were closely related to Rembrandt in subject matter. Lastman and Pynas belonged to a particular branch of the Caravaggesque trend, deriving from the German, Adam Elsheimer, whose drawings were of the highest importance for the formation of Rembrandt's mature style of pen drawing. The other trend distinguished itself by its expressiveness and owes its origins mainly to Jacques Callot, the great French etcher and draughtsman, who gained a tremendous influence on European graphic art in the second quarter of the seventeenth century. Callot's influence on Rembrandt's etchings has been observed already long ago, but it was marked also in the drawings, especially the technique of drawing and etching, and was much stronger than was generally assumed. The studies of old men, seated in brilliant or veiled light, are specimens of the Dutch Caravaggism and its pene- trating study of nature. All details in the wrinkled old faces, in the garments of heavy cloth are carefully described. It was the characteristic features that fascinated Rembrandt most in these subjects as they did in genre scenes with beggars and common people. The figures form compact clumps with closed outlines. In contrast to these types stand figures which flare up in a vertical direction (No. 1). Even when they were drawn from nature they incorporate a stylistic feeling which is essentially related to Callot's art. In the Raising of the Cross (No. 2), this becomes evident also for the whole composition with its vertically rising figures in the background. Callot was in the habit of giving his figures a flat relief by alternately thickening and thinning their contours.[1] We notice this kind of relief in Rembrandt's chalk drawings as well as in his pen drawings (Nos. 2, 6, 10).

We need not assume that those elongated, vertical forms, which are of Manneristic origin, were imparted to Rembrandt only through the works of Callot. We find them also in the works of Jan Pynas, which were highly appreciated and collected by Rembrandt.[2] The flamboyant manner of Callot was fused with the towering inven- tions of Pynas (Nos. 13, 15).

The two mentioned influences were, of course, only important in that they stimu- lated him to develop his innate aptitudes. The feeling for the heavy and earthbound on the one hand, the inclination for the spiritual and expressively transcendent on the other hand, are basic and lasting features of Rembrandt's art.

What was conventional and late Manneristic in the world of style Rembrandt derived from, was speedily changed by him into vigorous vision of nature. We observe this in the 'stormy' or mysteriously live line-work of his compositional projects. The emotional and visionary character of a figure like No. 11 cannot be traced back to models: it is original. In some of the drawings (Nos. 16, 22, 30) we notice the

[1]He demonstrated this especially in his model books for drawing instruction.

[2]Houbraken reports that Rembrandt passed through the studio of Jacob Pynas, the brother of Jan, after his apprenticeship with Lastman.

use of loops and flourishes, which are a convention of the Early Baroque, and of Manneristic descent. They do not degenerate to mere decorative calligraphy. They are soon counteracted by a violent and scratchy rhythm, full of intensely marked shadow accents (Nos. 10, 20), by stormy zig-zags and barbed hooks which almost pierce the paper (Nos. 17, 19). No spell of line could persuade Rembrandt to set aside what is characteristic, expressive, suggestive of space and light. Rembrandt achieved the acme of mastery of light in drawing. This imparts to his representations their unique naturalness. Considering the strong interest which the seventeenth century took in the mastery of nature, Rembrandt's drawings must have had the effect of revelations. In this respect, he surpassed by far his friend and studio companion, Jan Lievens, who approached him closely in mastery of composition, but never of the single figure.

As models for portrait studies, Rembrandt used mostly members of his family, or his own face (Nos. 5, 7, 8, 14). Some of these studies were done by artificial light. The physiognomic expression was the focus of interest for the young artist who did not hesitate even to exaggerate unpleasant features of his models in order to reach his aim.

Rembrandt's move to Amsterdam was brought about by his activity as a successful portrait painter. Besides, in painting and etching, large and small biblical compositions filled the first half of the 1630s. In drawing, the study from nature gained an ever increasing and broadening importance. The character figure and physiognomic study was replaced by the natural spell of the personality in portraits (Nos. 21, 22). The technical mastery of the means of representation was tremendously increased (No. 43). Rembrandt achieved greater precision in grasping the form; so he preferred the sharp pen to the blurred and less decisive chalk. His numerous studies from nature, and illustrative inventions are mostly executed with the quill-pen. In 1632–1633, the line-work of the pen keeps something still of the brittleness of the Callot-style of the Leiden years. This is particularly evident in the free inventions, where we often see a hooky angularity and ecstatically sweeping lines (Nos. 25, 29, 31). Occasionally, we even meet with Manneristic features (e.g. remembrances of the style of Fontainebleau in No. 28). These residua of an earlier formal convention were transformed by Rembrandt into means of his expressive diction. Also his studies from the life surrounding him were influenced by this style (Nos. 27, 33), especially if they seem to have been preparatory drawings. We can observe in mere studies from nature how quickly Rembrandt changed formulas of a linear convention into premissless observation of nature (Nos. 23, 34, 37, 39). This may even involve a certain disorder and disorganization of the linear system; the lines are sometimes scattered around like dispersed stalks. But faithfulness to nature was more important to Rembrandt than any preconceived formula. The washed fleck or area is always able to keep together the disconnected lines (No. 37) and to bring about the union with space, filled with the medium of atmosphere and light. The result is as close to nature as it is exemplary for the establishment of the Baroque style in drawing.

We frequently meet with sheets of sketches where figures and scenes from daily life cover the paper like a pattern (No. 73). This type of drawing, which Rembrandt first adapted also to etching, was introduced into art and recommended to young painters by Leonardo da Vinci. Among Rembrandt's precursors, Jacques de Gheyn especially cultivated it. After Rembrandt, Watteau was its greatest representative. Under Rembrandt's hands, these sheets of sketches acquired an incomparable psychical life (No. 38). Little comedies and tragedies grow there in the bud, proving what importance Rembrandt's studies from nature had for his narrative art.

Towards the middle of the 1630s, Rembrandt became increasingly engaged in problems of monumental historical painting. This was a culminating point in the Baroque phase of Rembrandt's art, which covers the years down to 'The Nightwatch'. Rembrandt outgrew only now the limitations of his Leiden years. Large sizes dominate his paintings, and we notice the reflection also among the drawings (No. 44). To be an artist of European importance in the seventeenth century was not possible without defining one's position in regard to Italian art, in painting as well as in music. Rembrandt did this with thoroughness. Caravaggism now came to his attention, not only through its Northern followers, but also through the sources. Rembrandt had the opportunity of seeing many Italian originals on the Dutch art market. Besides, he became acquainted with the works of the Flemish masters. The striving for plasticity of strong, vigorously moved bodies also fills his drawings (No. 49). To present dramatic action at its highest climax was a problem which attracted his foremost attention. The lines swing and whirl around the curved surfaces of the massive solids, and thus bring them into being. From the Baroque painters, Rembrandt proceeded to the masters of the High Renaissance, eager to know how they dealt with similar problems. Movement and emotion in the group of the Apostles fascinated him in Leonardo's Last Supper (Nos. 45, 46). The dated pen drawing determines chronologically a large group of pen drawings, the number of which increases astoundingly about the middle of the 1630s. The pen-lines seem to be split, dissolved into fibres in the violent play of motion and emotion (Nos. 47, 48). The eruption of wild movement, breaking out of deeply stirred souls, was never represented so convincingly as in Rembrandt's drawings of this time.

The numerous historical subjects of the middle of the 1630s are supplemented by a still larger number of scenes from everyday life in which Rembrandt followed up similar problems. He caught the expression of the moment: a smile, the playful or enraged movement of a little child, the friendly approach of a dog (Nos. 65, 66, 67), the dialogue of actors (No. 51), the devout listening to music (No. 53). Rembrandt was constantly observing at home and in the street. The long series of drawings entitled in Capelle's inventory 'Life of Women' came into being (Nos. 61–68). Pen-work is combined with layers of wash resulting in magnificent light and space effects (Nos. 40, 61, 62). Saskia is frequently the subject of the homely scenes.

The strong realism, which forms an essential part of the Caravaggesque manner, is another marked feature of these drawings. It comes to the fore in the plumpness and heaviness of the figures, which prevails in spite of the violent dynamism of the linear texture (No. 59). Studio models and his own image were endowed by Rembrandt with this quality (Nos. 77, 78).

The drawings of 1635 reveal a restlessness and breathlessness, which calmed down in the following years. The naturalism became less emotional, more descriptive, enjoying the graphic lines and flecks (compare No. 50 with No. 76). More contemplative subjects occur (Nos. 70–72). Even the home scenes acquire a radiant stateliness (No. 79). Landscape entered Rembrandt's circle of subjects, and several brilliant drawings of Dutch motives originated (Nos. 74, 75).

With 1637, a new, strong principle of style arose, a certain withdrawing from the unlimited realism of 1635, a striving towards abstraction. This tendency lasted until the end of the decade. It again took up the angular character of the Callot-style of the 1620s and the early 1630s, but lent it a new tectonic firmness, sometimes going so far as to give the figures a mechanic, armoured aspect. We notice this angular, cubic rhythm in copies after Lastman (No. 82), in historical compositions (Nos. 90, 97), but even in studies from nature (No. 87), and portraits (No. 81). A new occurrence of the tendency towards the strange, fantastic, transcendent and expressive is noticeable (Nos. 92–94). Rembrandt seems to look for the picturesque and eccentric also in daily life. It is an outspoken tendency, but did not prevent Rembrandt from proceeding at the same time with the most admirable and refreshing studies from nature (Nos. 83, 84, 86), proving his tremendous progress in mastering colour values through the medium of black and white.

The 1630s conclude with a synthesis of the dynamic movement of 1635 and the newly gained structural firmness (Nos. 104, 110). The clarification and abstraction of form allowed Rembrandt to discard the multitude of split pen-strokes, and to make serpentine lines of dynamic energy shoot along the shapes, penetrating space into all directions.

In the usual division of Rembrandt's career into periods, the 1640s are considered the middle period. About 1641–1642 was a turning-point in Rembrandt's development. The bold Baroque penetration of space came to a climax and, in some ways, also to an end. The new tectonic firmness, displayed by Rembrandt not only in the representation of cities and buildings (Nos. 112, 115), but also in compositional projects (Nos. 119, 120), lead to a general calming down. The vehement movement slowed up. A premonition of the mature style occasionally occurs in technique (No. 120) as well as in invention (No. 118). This applies also to the paintings, which unfold a new beauty of colour and light. Landscape is a suitable carrier of such values, therefore it entered Rembrandt's picture subjects in broad stream, in painting, etching, and drawing (Nos. 113–116, 133B, 134).

Two qualities are predominant in the production of the 1640s: the striving for pictorial totality, and the quieting and deepening of the content.

The striving for a painterly effect, the occupation with problems of light and colour brought it about that Rembrandt frequently changed the diction of his style of drawing. The style of the 1640s, therefore, was not so easily recognized as that of the 1630s and 1650s. The systematization of line plays a lesser part in it. The pen-stroke has lost its hurrying, violent dynamism. Lines go in quiet curves, sliding, turning, and returning, circumscribing coloured surfaces (Nos. 125, 129, 130). Rembrandt liked in these years to embed the line-work into the rich flowing clouds of washes, to give the drawings pictorial unity (Nos. 124, 132). The same sensibility for colour values is betrayed by the frequent use of black chalk for figure and landscape studies, over which a greyish silvery hue of air seems to be spread (Nos. 126, 127, 135, 138, 142, 143). The quiet, thoughtful and intimate distinguishes Rembrandt's picture narrations, whether they are of religious (No. 139) or of profane (No. 131) content.

The flowing diffusion of line was soon given up for a new intensification, which became noticeable first of all in compositional projects. Rembrandt gradually developed a simplicity which enabled him to lay down in a few striking traits the very essence and spiritual meaning of a composition (Nos. 137, 140, 141, 144, 146). The lines incline to thicken—a tendency already to be observed at the beginning of the 1640s, but then still in combination with curly flourishes. Now the vigorous and saturated main lines are ready to do the whole work, and flourishes are discarded as superfluous. Therewith Rembrandt's drawing style entered a new phase, the beginning maturity, which prepared the style of the 1650s. In the basic traits of drawings which obtained a more lavish pictorial execution, too, this new vigour comes to the fore, and lends them a force which is more subtly organized than the rough power of the 1630s (Nos. 147, 148).

Even drawings with large figure crowds avoid all curliness and confusion in the second half of the 1640s (Nos. 157, 158). The proportions of the figures become shorter: the form of a V-shaped angle frequently occurs in the rhythm of the pen-lines. Space expands in solemn width.

How Rembrandt indicates *colour* as the main substance, and thus penetrates the surface, giving more of the soul of the object, is most evident in his landscape drawings. A new prolific era of landscape drawing begins in the late 1640s, and some of the favourite motives of Rembrandt's maturity appear for the first time (No. 154). The verticals and horizontals are emphasized. The scenery expands in horizontal bands where everything is fused and unified in the optical plane of the distance (No. 153). The drawings of old towns and buildings not only render picturesque motives, but give more: the sentiment of past times, of a declined world, the secret beauty of ruin and decay.

The figure drawings of the end of the 1640s betray an increasing tendency towards clearness and the developing of sculpturesque qualities (Nos. 159, 160, 163, 164, 167). Curves and waves turn into straight lines. Radiant layers of parallel hatches increase the colourful richness of the firm compositions. We stand at the threshold of Rembrandt's late period.

The 1650s, the period of Rembrandt's highest maturity, signify also the acme of his art of drawing. Rembrandt formulated his classical style in this decade, which became also the classical era of Dutch art in general. The number of drawings which Rembrandt did in the 1650s surpassed that of any other period. Studies from life decrease considerably in comparison with the previous periods. Instead, there is a tremendous growth in free inventions of historical and narrative content. Rembrandt mastered the latter with greatest freedom and ease, as if he had seen them in reality. Landscape drawing had now its richest and most splendid development.

It is customary to consider the 1650s and 1660s as one great period, 'the late period', in the art of Rembrandt. Our modern time, according to its own artistic convictions, gives it the greatest praise, while the eighteenth century was fascinated by the early Rembrandt. If we study the drawings, we shall find it difficult to make a break at the beginning of the 1650s. Especially the group of landscapes, but also the figure drawings reveal a continuous transition from the end of the 1640s into the 1650s. We have to proceed to the 1660s in order to find so profound a change as at the beginning of the 1640s. If a point of origin for the ideas of 1650 should be indicated, we shall find it rather at about 1648.

The early 1650s were the years of Rembrandt's most intensive study of landscape. On various excursions in the surroundings of Amsterdam, he collected a multitude of motives[1] which served him as inspirations for his etchings,[2] sometimes also as elements of their composition (Nos. 170, 172, 177, 179). While the drawings of the 1630s favoured the effect of the vehemently contrasting blotch, and those of the 1640s the effect of richly enveloping areas of shadowy washes, the drawings of the 1650s employed only very light washes, or such of a medium intensity, as if they were filled with reflections of light. The atmospheric continuity which Rembrandt achieved in these drawings

[1]Many of them were successfully identified by Frits Lugt in his book Mit Rembrandt in Amsterdam, Berlin, 1920.

[2]Half of Rembrandt's landscape etchings were done from 1650 to 1652.

was never surpassed in art. He realized only now the majestic immensity of the Dutch scenery. In its endless expanse of space, the most modest motive achieves a particular monumentality (No. 176). The pen-work has a greater importance than ever, because it remains clearly visible and is never drowned by shadows. It consists either of thin, whizzing lines, recalling the structure of some etchings (Nos. 170, 174), or of stronger ones with larger intervals (Nos. 172, 175), or of vibrating bands of delicate short hatches, interspersed with slightly curving hair-lines (Nos. 177, 179, 181). We notice that Rembrandt had successfully studied the drawings by the Venetian masters of the Titian circle[1] and by Pieter Bruegel.

Rembrandt turned definitely away from the Baroque ideals of his youth, from movement and sharp accents, from emphasized characteristic and dramatic emotion. His art became quiet and silent, concentrated on the essential in great, simple forms, discovering the internal structure of spirit and existence. This is true of his single figures as much (No. 168) as it is of whole compositions (Nos. 186, 187). In spite of the parsimonious application of washes, the colourful brilliancy grows (No. 184). The figures have the tendency towards crystallizing in cubic forms. The lines are straight, the links articulated. The brittle reed-pen is the best suitable instrument for those frail and splintery lines. About 1652, there originated a whole group of drawings which show strokes of extreme lightness, airiness, and luminosity (Nos. 189–192).

Rembrandt more and more approached classical models and classical concepts (Nos. 195, 196), because they coincided with his liking for the quiet, thoughtful, and monumental. The masters of the Italian High Renaissance, and the figures of Greek and Roman antiquity impressed him deeply; a fact which gives the lie to the complaints of his classicist critics. Rembrandt's relation to the classic world was much more profound than that of the superficial academicians.

Towards the middle of the decade, the geometrization of figure composition increased (Nos. 199–206, 211). Curves were avoided. The figures are now composed of cubes, rhombus and cylinder forms, and have clearly crystallized shape. Sometimes their abstractness gives them the appearance of articulated dolls. Yet they are far from being lifeless. On the contrary, the simplicity of their shape and their external immobility increase their inward emotion. The faces are typical, but the attitude of their bodies reveals their feelings. In similar manner, only by the rhythms of pure line, the alternation of strong and fine strokes, without supporting washes, Rembrandt gives the perfect illusion of space and light—one of the greatest secrets of his late art.

This mode of drawing was not the only one adopted by Rembrandt about the middle of the decade. A group of pen-drawings (Nos. 207–210, 212) equals the

[1]No. 182 and the etching to which it is preparatory betray a knowledge of Campagnola.

paintings of the time in glistening colour effect. The incoherent lines of the reed-pen, varyingly saturated with the medium, flash up in space like the sparkling colour phenomena thrown on the canvas with half-dry brush.

The most advanced group of landscape drawings between 1653 and 1655 gives the utmost in illusion of space, light, and atmosphere. The surface of the paper, set in contrast to light layers of washes, attains a radiant quality of its own (No. 214). Not only the specific mood, the most subtle spell of light are caught (No. 228), but also the breath of the elements: the moving of trees in the wind sweeping over the canals and polders (Nos. 221, 224), the humidity of the air penetrating everything with a faint haze and making the simplest motive appear in a remote and mysterious grandeur (No. 223). The pen-strokes often give a shorthand indication of the main accents only, which enlivens the expressiveness of the subject in a unique way (No. 220).

Rembrandt's universal mind became absorbed in the form and spirit of works of art of remote centuries and regions. In copies from Indian miniatures, he tried to revive the colouristic and linear spell of the works of the old oriental painters (Nos. 229–232).[1] We notice the influence of these studies also in inventions of his own (No. 233). The solemnity of a composition of the Raphael circle inspired Rembrandt to recast it in drawings (No. 265). The severe linear system of a Mantegna drawing tempted him to emulation (No. 241). Its parallel hatches occur in a group of studies from nature (Nos. 238, 239, 251), among them the master's famous Self-Portrait (No. 250). Those rays of parallels which have in the Italian original the purpose of emphasizing the tactile relief blend Rembrandt's figures into an optical plane, the result of the depth of atmospheric space which surrounds them. Vigorous studies from nature, done with reed-pen or brush (Nos. 245–251), embed the figures into a fluid which enhances and aggrandizes them; the majestic planelike simplicity of their silhouette is suggestive of the depth of space behind them. Within great outlining strokes extends the soft relief of nude studies like a membrane (No. 242). All these drawings reveal the same highly pictorial qualities as the contemporary paintings, so akin in spirit to Titian. The broad strokes of reed-pen and drawing brush have fluorescent power equal to the broad brush-work in the paintings.

In the art of the late Rembrandt, we observe increasingly the antinomy of two artistic principles which do not exclude each other, but go parallel and contribute equally to the incomparable richness of this art: synthesis and dissolution. We notice a strong tectonic and plastic will at work at the same time as the highest pictorial spiritualization and dissolution. Drawings like Nos. 253, 254, 257 vibrate in the trembling life of radiant lines, which lend them not only the fluorescence of colour, but also a diaphanous quality as if the life of the soul would sublimate the bodies,

[1] The light stroke of his pen approaches drawings by the Persian master Riza Abashi.

Awe and majesty (No. 253), love and faithful devotion (No. 257) are expressed by those long and raylike lines in a most touching way. In No. 254, we see also clearly the tendency to blocklike tightening which is so significant of the late style of Rembrandt. Yet the blocks are of no material heaviness. We notice this in drawings like Nos. 255 and 256. Even the figures assume short, square proportions, but what a spiritual lightness and intensity of narration is expressed by those cumbrous beings! How does the drawing radiate from an inner, mysterious light, spread by the figure of Christ!

Blocklike tightening makes of the figures sculpturesque solids (Nos. 258–260), which in their silent concentration are filled with immense psychical life. These drawings are accompanied by others, which are of a mysterious vibrancy (Nos. 263–265), caused by the broad strokes of the reed-pen, frequently intermittent and leaving faint scratchy marks on the paper: a summum of dematerialization and spiritualization.

Studies from the nude and landscapes (Nos. 261, 262) are now an exception; they attain the ultimate in simplified and monumental rendering of nature and substance, in saturation with colour and light.

In some drawings of the end of the decade (Nos. 270–273), the figures have the grandeur of monuments. They are set on the paper in thick lines as if they were cut in stone. The meaning of those lines is not that of a heavily marked separation from the mysterious medium of space. On the contrary, it means all the more intensive union with the atmosphere. The atmosphere is, so to say, banked up on the figures' outlines and becomes visible in dark borders. The figures, on the other hand, change their substance and become embodiments of atmospheric space, now more a metaphysical medium than a physical one.

Of the 1660s, the last period of Rembrandt's activity, there are but a few drawings known. This is not due to the fact that there have been less drawings preserved, although Rembrandt may have been more careless in keeping his drawings, which he sometimes sketched on the backs of printed leaflets, but rather because drawing with pen and brush on paper as a technical process lost some of its previous importance for Rembrandt.[1] Yet the old Rembrandt put the immediateness of drawing, of handwriting into the technique of his paintings, which his contemporaries, therefore, considered as 'unfinished'. Painting and drawing approach each other closer than ever before. The studies for the Self-Portrait in the Louvre (No. 292) and the Staalmeesters (Nos. 281, 282) contain in their radiating power the complete idea of the pictorial totality. Some of the drawings are executed with brush and pen, and work with body-colours and erasures. All graphic system has been abandoned. No. 276 is of an iridescent texture, a waving of shadow and light, out of which the figures

---

[1] For the same reason etching disappeared from his production after 1661.

rise like visions. Some drawings, on the other hand, show an immense structural firmness (Nos. 284, 288).

The very last drawings (Nos. 289–291) cannot be dated exactly to a year, because we lack every chain of development. The broad, simplified outlines begin anew to fluctuate, to oscillate. The vibration of the split pen-strokes, of the floating washes, make all bulk diaphanous, dissolve all solid forms. But the result is no decomposition, as, on the other hand, space and atmospheric fluid show the tendency to crystallize. In this way, a firmness is attained which greatly surpasses all the earlier works. Rembrandt's last word, also in drawing, is to lay bare the innermost laws of existence.

THE PROBLEM OF CRITICISM

THE problem of criticism is one of the most difficult with regard to Rembrandt's drawings. Rembrandt's teaching activity was considerable. He educated generations of pupils, who did not give up their personality in such a high degree as the pupils of Rubens, but, nevertheless, approached the master so closely that it is sometimes hard to draw the line of discrimination.

The criticism of Rembrandt's drawings has to be based on objective and reliable foundations. These are first of all given by the drawings, very few in number, which are signed or inscribed by the master himself. Equal documentary evidence is given by the larger number of drawings preparatory to etchings or paintings. Those two groups give the primary documentary evidence, a stock of work upon which we can rely under any circumstances. Whatever other drawings we may assume to be works by Rembrandt cannot be without relation to this basic stock.

Among the vast number of drawings attributed to Rembrandt, there is a very considerable group which is so outstanding in quality that the authorship of the master is self-evident. Yet the point of quality is too subjective to form the only basis for attribution to Rembrandt. Because of the outstanding quality of some work done by pupils in Rembrandt's studio, it may even happen that an especially attractive drawing by a disciple overshadows less significant works of the master. Therefore, every drawing ascribed to Rembrandt must stand the test of being brought into plausible relation with the basic stock of work mentioned before, and with the ascertained paintings and etchings. The same kind of structure, the same feeling for texture must unite them.

Discrimination on the basis of quality will not be difficult in the case when both a drawing by the master and its copy by a pupil are preserved. Real freedom and imitation of freedom can easily be distinguished for inner and outer reasons. Faint preliminary strokes with black lead are indicative of the pupil's work in such a case.

Another objective basis of testing a drawing will be its ability to be included in the chronological sequence of the genuine drawings without contradiction. As Rembrandt kept most of his drawings in his studio, works from different phases were available as material of instruction for the school. Consequently, the pupils occasionally combined in one and the same drawing features characteristic of different periods of Rembrandt.

There is no mechanical way of testing the genuineness of a Rembrandt drawing. Subjective consideration can never be eliminated, but we can try to control it as much as possible by objective reasons. These reasons, of course, can be worked out successfully only in intimate acquaintance with the drawings themselves. In this regard, connoisseurship is indispensable. The scholar occupied with research on Rembrandt drawings has to know them from autopsy. Photographs and reproductions easily deceive. Many a drawing which gave rise to no doubts in a photograph had to be discarded when seen in reality. On the other hand, many a doubtful drawing had to be restored to Rembrandt's œuvre because the autopsy revealed a genuine drawing reworked by another hand—a case which can only be decided before the original.

PLATES

I

THE LEIDEN PERIOD

Plates 1–20

II

FROM THE MOVE TO AMSTERDAM TO THE BEGINNING OF THE HUNDRED GUILDER PRINT

Plates 21–110

III

FROM THE NIGHTWATCH TO THE STAALMEESTERS

Plates 111–282

IV

THE LAST YEARS

Plates 283–292

All measurements are given in millimetres

An asterisk (*) in front of the number indicates that
the reproduction is in the same size as the original

1. STUDY OF AN ARCHER. About 1627. Dresden, Kupferstichkabinett.
(Red chalk, 306 : 162)

*2. THE RAISING OF THE CROSS. About 1627/28. Rotterdam, F. Koenigs Collection.
(Black chalk, 193 : 148)

3. OLD MAN WITH A BOOK. Study for the Philosophers in Melbourne, 1628. Berlin, Kupferstichkabinett.
(Red and black chalk, 295 : 210)

4. A FOOT OPERATION. About 1628. Florence, Uffizi.
(Chalk, pen and wash, 317 : 266)

*5. REMBRANDT'S MOTHER. About 1628/29. Lausanne, A. Stroelin.
(Pen and brush, 120 : 105)

*6. JUDAS REPENTANT. Study for the painting mentioned in the autobiography of C. Huyghens. About 1629.
Formerly Vienna, Albertina. (Pen and wash, 112 : 145)

*8. SELF-PORTRAIT. About 1628/29. Spiez, J. de Bruijn.
(Pen and wash, 127 : 95)

*7. SELF-PORTRAIT. About 1627/28. London, British Museum.
(Pen and wash, 127 : 95)

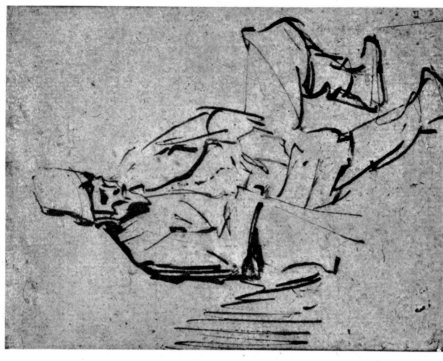

*10. A SEATED MAN IN HIGH CAP. About 1629. Rotterdam, Museum Boymans. (Pen, 120 : 92)

*9. A BEGGAR-WOMAN. About 1628/29. Jenkintown, Pa., Alverthorpe Gallery. (Pen and brush, 135 : 120)

*11. STUDY FOR THE FIGURE OF ST. PETER IN THE ETCHING B.95. About 1629. Dresden, Kupferstichkabinett.
(Black chalk, 254 : 190)

12. ST. PAUL. Preparatory drawing for the Etching B.149. About 1629. Paris, Louvre.
(Red chalk and wash, 236 : 201)

*14. REMBRANDT'S FATHER. About 1630. Oxford, Ashmolean Museum. (Red and black chalk, wash, 189 : 240)

15. THE ENTOMBMENT OF CHRIST. Dated 1630. London, British Museum.
(Red chalk, 280 : 203)

16. SEATED OLD MAN, BOWED FORWARD. Preparatory drawing for the
etching B.325 of 1630. Stockholm, Nationalmuseum. (Red chalk)

*17. SEATED OLD MAN, THREE-QUARTER-LENGTH. Dated 1630. Jenkintown, Pa., Alverthorpe Gallery.
(Red chalk, 157 : 147)

*18. OLD MAN SEATED IN AN ARM-CHAIR, TURNED TOWARDS THE RIGHT. Dated 1631.
Haarlem, Museum Teyler. (Red and black chalk, 225 : 145)

*19. OLD MAN WITH CLASPED HANDS, SEATED IN AN ARM-CHAIR. Study used for the painting of 1633,
A Scholar seated in an Interior, Louvre. Berlin, Kupferstichkabinett. (Red and black chalk, 226 : 157)

*20. OLD MAN IN A HIGH CAP, SEATED IN PROFILE TO THE RIGHT. About 1631.
Paris, Louvre. E. de Rothschild Bequest. (Pen and wash, 152 : 128)

*21.   PORTRAIT OF SASKIA IN A STRAW-HAT.   Dated June 8, 1633.
Berlin, Kupferstichkabinett.   (Silver-point, 185 : 107)

*23. AN OLD MAN AND A YOUNG WOMAN WALKING.
About 1632/33. Dresden, Kupferstichkabinett. (Pen, 149 : 98)

*22. PORTRAIT OF SASKIA, SEATED IN AN ARM-CHAIR. About 1633.
Paris, Louvre. (Red chalk, 147 : 110)

*25. CHRIST CONVERSING WITH MARY IN THE HOUSE OF LAZARUS.
About 1632/33. Zurich, Dr. Charles Simon. (Pen. 125 : 110)

*24. SELF-PORTRAIT. About 1633. Marseilles, Musée des Beaux-Arts.
(Black chalk, 110 : 110)

*26. STUDY FOR LOT DRUNK. Dated 1633. Connected with a painting done in the Leiden period. Frankfort-on-Main, Städelsches Kunstinstitut. (Black chalk, 251 : 189)

*27. AN ORIENTAL STANDING. About 1633. London, British Museum.
(Pen and wash, 221 : 169)

*28. GROUP FOR AN ENTOMBMENT OF CHRIST. About 1632/33. Berlin, Kupferstichkabinett.
(Pen, 124 : 149)

*29. THE TEMPTATION OF CHRIST. About 1632/33. Frankfort-on-Main, Städelsches Kunstinstitut. (Pen, 126 : 161)

*30. THE RAISING OF THE CROSS. Preparatory drawing for the painting of 1633, The Raising of the Cross, Munich. Vienna, Albertina.
(Black chalk and wash, 232 : 187)

*31. THE RAISING OF THE DAUGHTER OF JAIRUS. About 1632/33. Rotterdam, F. Koenigs Collection. (Pen, 188 : 240)

*32.   THE LAMENTATION FOR CHRIST.   About 1632/33.   Dresden, Kupferstichkabinett.   (Pen, 182 : 260)

*33. AN ARTIST IN HIS STUDIO (PROBABLY REMBRANDT HIMSELF).   About 1632/33.   London (Chelsea), L. H. Walters.
(Pen, 205 : 170)

*34. TWO WOMEN TEACHING A CHILD TO WALK. About 1632/33. F. Lugt Collection.
(Pen and wash, 160 : 144)

*35. A WATCH-DOG SLEEPING IN HIS HUTCH. About 1633. Paris, Lucien Guiraud.
(Pen and wash, 130 : 153)

*36. THE ENTRANCE OF A COTTAGE WITH A DRAW-WELL. Study after nature, used for the etching B.90 of 1633. Hamburg, Kunsthalle. (Pen and wash, 180 : 233)

*37. YOUNG WOMAN AT HER TOILET. About 1632/34. Vienna, Albertina. (Pen and wash, 238 : 184)

*38. STUDIES OF BEGGARS AND OF AN OLD WOMAN WITH A CRYING CHILD. About 1633/34. Berlin, Kupferstichkabinett.
(Pen, 218 : 186)

*39.   TWO STUDIES OF A YOUNG WOMAN READING.   About 1633/34.   New York, Courtesy of the
Metropolitan Museum of Art. (Pen, 173 : 150)

*40. SASKIA SEATED BY A WINDOW. About 1634. F. Lugt Çollection.
(Pen and wash, 170 : 125)

*41. BEARDED OLD MAN, HALF-LENGTH. Dated 1634.
The Hague, Royal Library. (Pen and wash, 89 : 71)

*42. SASKIA HAVING HER HAIR COMBED. About 1634.
F. Lugt Collection. (Pen, 198 : 100)

43. PORTRAIT OF A MAN IN AN ARM-CHAIR, SEEN THROUGH A WINDOW-FRAME. Dated 1634. New York, Mrs. Charles S. Payson.
(Red and black chalk, pen and wash, 373 : 272)

44. JESUS AND HIS DISCIPLES. Dated 1634. Haarlem, Museum Teyler. (Black and red chalk, pen and wash, gouache, 355 : 476)

45. THE LAST SUPPER, AFTER LEONARDO DA VINCI. About 1635. Dresden, Friedrich August II. (Red chalk, 365 : 475)

46. THE LAST SUPPER, AFTER LEONARDO DA VINCI. Dated 1635. Berlin, Kupferstichkabinett.
(Pen, 128 : 385)

*47. CHRIST CARRYING THE CROSS. About 1635. Berlin, Kupferstichkabinett.
(Pen and wash, 145 : 260)

*48. THE ANNUNCIATION. About 1635. Besançon, Musée Communal.
(Pen, 144 : 124)

*49. ABRAHAM'S SACRIFICE. Preparatory drawing for the painting of 1635 in Leningrad.
London, British Museum. (Red and black chalk, wash, 194 : 146)

*50. STUDY FOR THE ETCHING OF 1635 B.340, THE GREAT JEWISH BRIDE. Stockholm, Nationalmuseum.
(Pen and wash, 232 : 182)

*51. AN ACTOR IN DIALOGUE WITH A KNEELING MAN. About 1635. Spiez, J. de Bruijn.
(Pen and wash, 182 : 153)

*52. THE CALVARY. About 1635. Berlin, Kupferstichkabinett. (Pen and wash. 218 : 179)

*53. GROUP OF MUSICIANS LISTENING TO A FLUTE PLAYER. About 1635. Newbury, Berkshire, Donnington Priory, G. M. Gathorne-Hardy. (Pen and wash, 135 : 154)

*54. JOSEPH EXPOUNDING THE PRISONERS' DREAMS. About 1635.
Basel, C. A. de Burlet. (Pen, 114 : 111)

*55. ST. PETER AND ST. JOHN HEALING THE PARALYSED AT THE GATE OF THE TEMPLE.
About 1635. Darmstadt, Hessisches Landesmuseum. (Pen, 121 : 172)

*56. THE PANCAKE WOMAN. About 1635. Amsterdam, Rijksprentenkabinet.
(Pen, 107 : 142)

*57. THE PROPHET ELIJAH AND THE WIDOW OF ZAREPHATH. CHILD WITH A DOG, used for the
Etching of 1635 B.124, The Pancake Woman. Paris, Louvre, Bonnat Bequest. (Pen, 117 : 159)

*59. SCRIBE SHARPENING HIS QUILL BY CANDLE-LIGHT. About 1635. Weimar, Grossherzogliches Museum. (Pen and wash, 125 : 123)

*58. BEARDED ORIENTAL IN A TURBAN, HALF-LENGTH. About 1635. Berlin, Kupferstichkabinett. (Pen and wash, 117 : 114)

*60. TWO BUTCHERS AT WORK. About 1635. Frankfort-on-Main, Städelsches Kunstinstitut. (Pen, 149 : 200)

*61. THREE WOMEN AT THE ENTRANCE OF A HOUSE, SEEN FROM THE INSIDE. About 1635. Bayonne, Musée, Collection Bonnat.
(Brush, Pen and wash, 250 : 190)

62. SASKIA LYING IN BED, AND A NURSE. About 1635. Munich, Graphische Sammlung.
(Brush, pen and wash, 328 : 165)

*63. SICK WOMAN LYING IN BED, PROBABLY SASKIA. About 1635. Paris, Petit Palais,
Collection Dutuit. (Pen and wash, 163 : 145)

*64. THE VIRGIN AND CHILD SEATED NEAR A WINDOW. About 1635. London, British Museum.
(Pen and wash, 155 : 137)

*65. MOTHER AND CHILD, FRIGHTENED BY A DOG. About 1635.
F. Lugt Collection. (Pen, 105 : 101)

66. WOMAN WITH FIVE CHILDREN PLAYING ON THE GROUND. About 1635. Bremen. Kunsthalle.
(Pen)

*67. THE NAUGHTY BOY. About 1635. Berlin, Kupferstichkabinett.
(Pen and wash, 206 : 143)

*69. MAN IN PLUMED HAT AND RICH COSTUME. About 1635/36. London,
Courtesy of the Victoria and Albert Museum. (Pen and wash, 160 : 105)

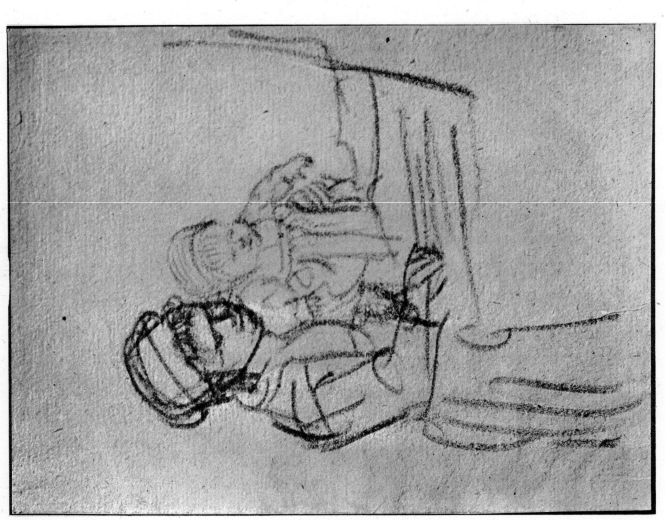

*68. NURSE AND CHILD. About 1635. Lwów, Lubomirski Museum.
(Red chalk, 178 : 128)

*70. DIANA WITH TWO GREYHOUNDS. About 1635/36. Basel, Dr. T. Christ. (Pen and wash, 183 : 263)

*71. ST. AUGUSTINE IN HIS STUDY. About 1635/36. Chatsworth, The Duke of Devonshire.
(Pen, 183 : 150)

*72. OLD MAN IN FLAT CAP SEATED ON A STEP. About 1636. New York, Courtesy of the
Metropolitan Museum of Art. (Pen and wash, 147 : 137)

73. SHEET OF STUDIES WITH NINE DIFFERENT HEADS AND HALF-LENGTH FIGURES.
About 1636. London, Heirs of Sir Henry Oppenheimer. (Pen and wash, red chalk, 220 : 233)

*74. COURT-YARD OF A FARM-HOUSE. About 1636. Budapest, Museum of Fine Arts. (Pen and wash, 164 : 226)

*75. ROW OF TREES IN AN OPEN FIELD. About 1636. Vienna, Akademie der Bildenden Künste. (Pen and wash, 133 : 244)

*76. WOMAN SEATED, IN ORIENTAL COSTUME. About 1636. Berlin, Kupferstichkabinett.
(Brush, pen and wash, 200 : 162)

77. LIFE-STUDY OF A YOUNG MAN PULLING A ROPE. About 1636. Amsterdam, Rijksprentenkabinet,
Hofstede de Groot Bequest. (Brush, pen and wash, 290 : 178)

*78. SELF-PORTRAIT. About 1636. New York, Dr. A. Hamilton Rice.
(Pen and wash, 145 : 121)

*79. SASKIA CARRYING RUMBARTUS DOWN STAIRS. About 1636. New York,
Courtesy of the Pierpont Morgan Library. (Pen and wash, 185 : 133)

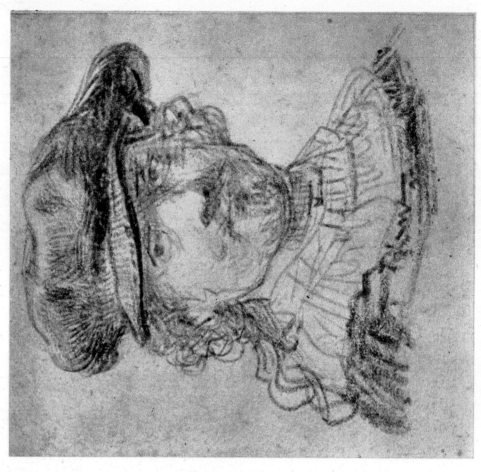

*81. SELF-PORTRAIT. About 1637. Jenkintown, Pa., Alverthorpe Gallery.
(Red Chalk, 129 : 119)

*80. MAN IN PLUMED HAT WITH A HALBERD.
About 1636/37. London, Victor Koch. (Pen, 85 : 72)

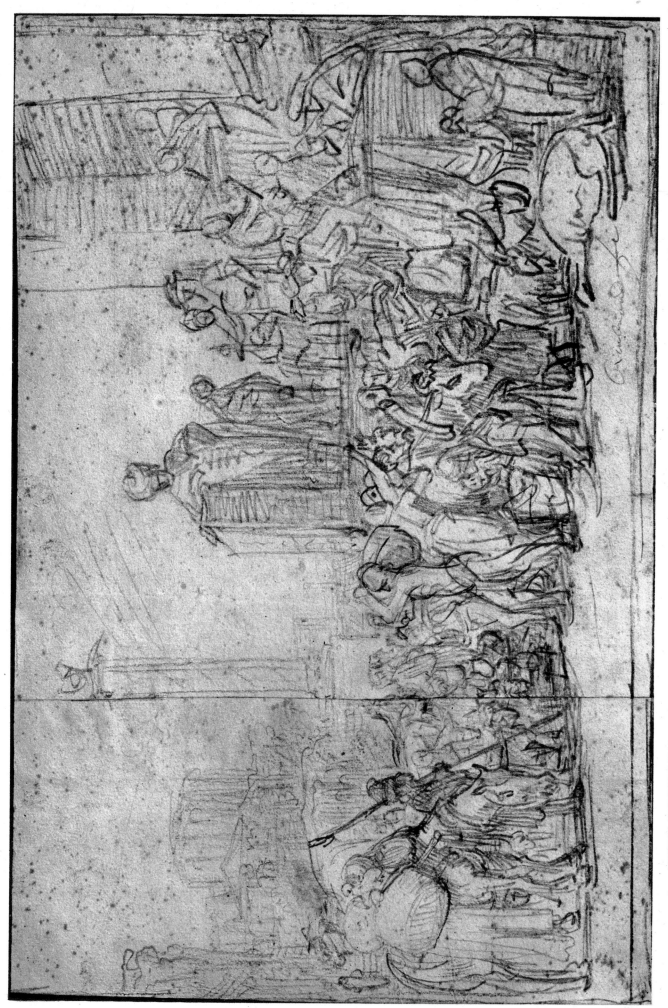

82. JOSEPH DISTRIBUTING GRAIN IN EGYPT. Copy after a painting by Pieter Lastman. About 1637. Vienna, Albertina. (Black chalk, 317 : 404)

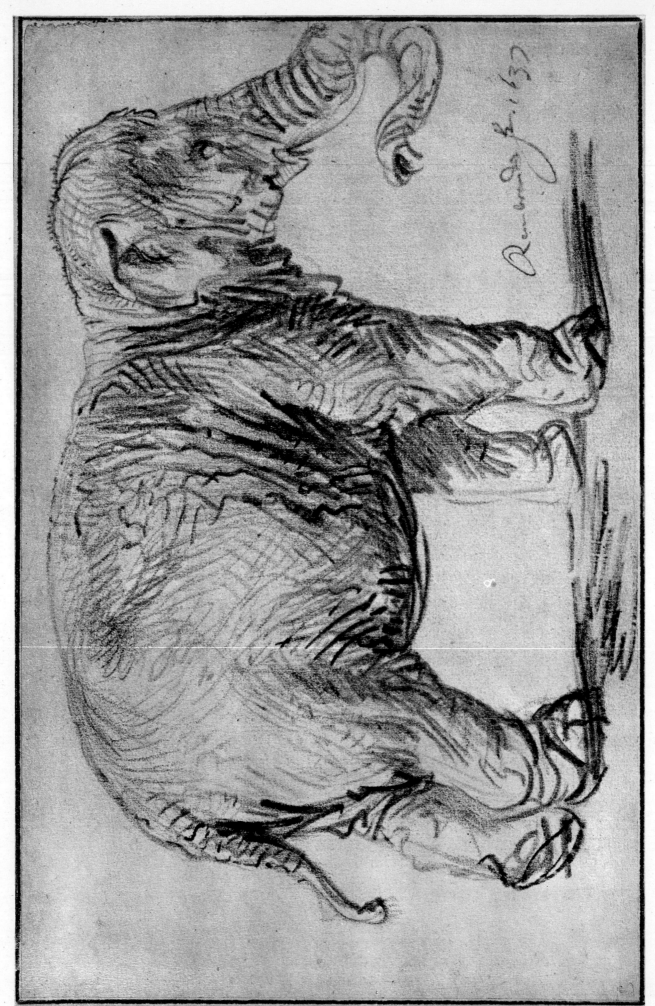

83. AN ELEPHANT. Dated 1637. Vienna, Albertina. (Black chalk, 230 : 340)

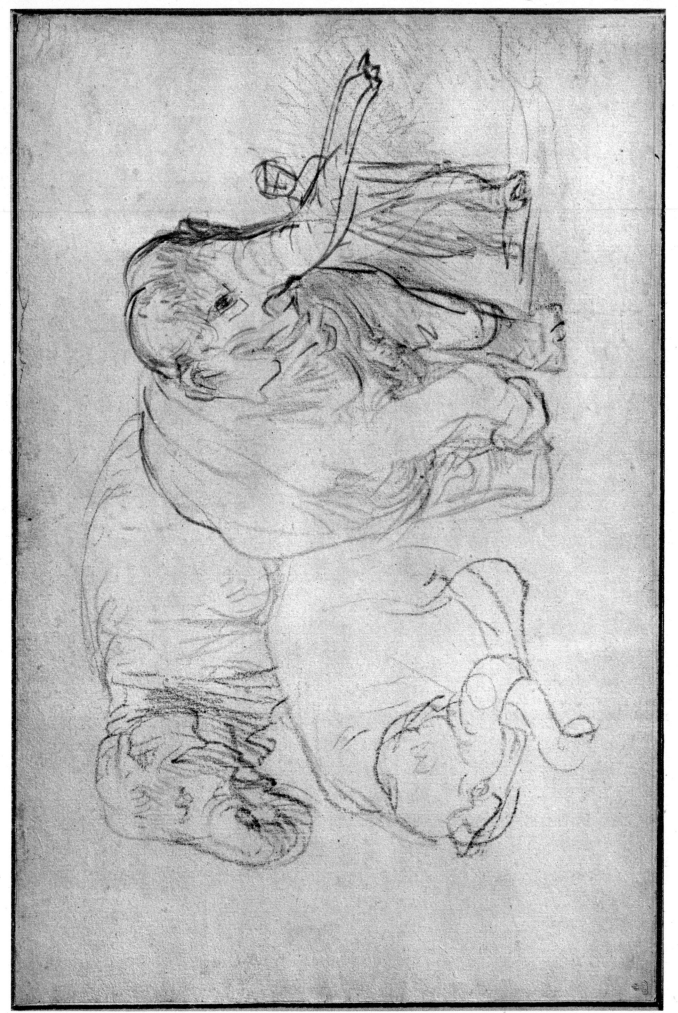

84. GROUP OF THREE ELEPHANTS. About 1637. Vienna, Albertina. (Black chalk, 242 : 363)

*85. FEMALE NUDE WITH A SNAKE (PROBABLY CLEOPATRA). About 1637.
London, O. Gutekunst. (Red chalk, 245 : 140)

*86.   SEATED GIRL IN PROFILE TO THE LEFT, HALF-NUDE.   About 1637.
Rotterdam, F. Koenigs Collection.   (Black chalk and white body-colour, 199 : 153)

*87. TWO NEGRO DRUMMERS MOUNTED ON MULES. About 1637. London, British Museum.
(Pen, wash, red chalk, water colour, 229 : 171)

*88. NEGRO BAND. About 1637. London, Victor Koch.
(Pen, wash, red and yellow chalk, 180 : 133)

*89. A QUACK ADDRESSING THE CROWD AT A FAIR. About 1637. Dresden, Friedrich August II.
(Pen and wash, 188 : 167)

90. SOLOMON'S IDOLATRY. About 1637. Paris, Louvre. (Red chalk, 485 : 376)

*91. DIFFERENT LISTENERS. Studies for the painting in Berlin, St. John the Baptist preaching.
About 1637. Berlin, Kupferstichkabinett. (Pen, 190 : 125)

*92. STUDIES OF A MATER DOLOROSA AND OF OTHER MOURNERS BENEATH THE CROSS. About 1637.
Amsterdam, Buma Collection. (Pen and red chalk, 200 : 140)

*93. DIFFERENT STUDIES FOR GROUPS AND FIGURES in the painting in Berlin, St. John the Baptist preaching. About 1637.
Berlin, Kupferstichkabinett. (Pen, 167 : 196)

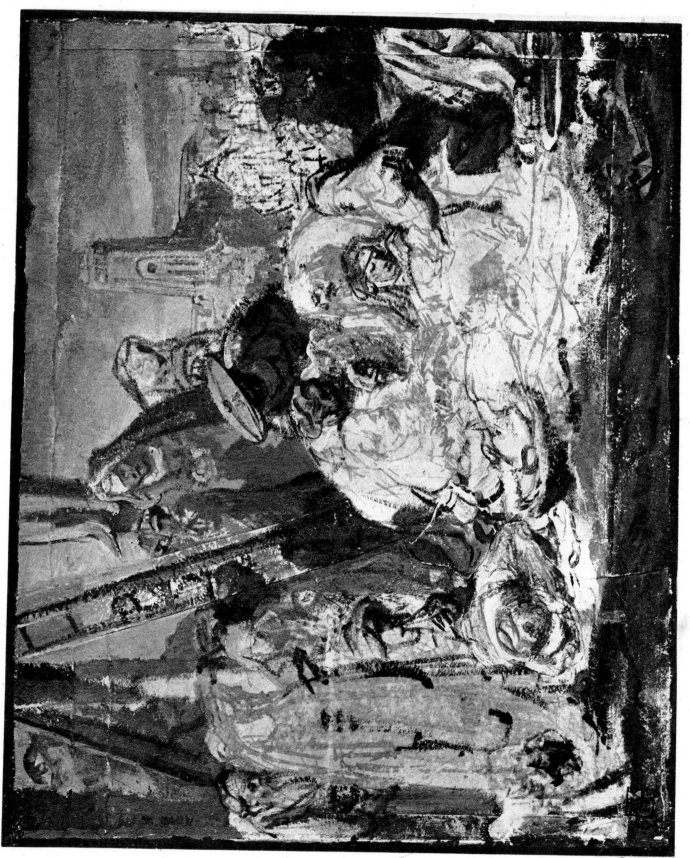

94. THE LAMENTATION FOR CHRIST. Preparatory drawing for the painting in London. About 1637/38. London, British Museum. (Pen, red and black chalk, wash, oil colour, 216 : 253)

*96. WOMAN CARRYING A CHILD, AND MAN IN FUR CAP. About 1637/38.
Besançon, Musée Communal. (Pen and wash, 140 : 118)

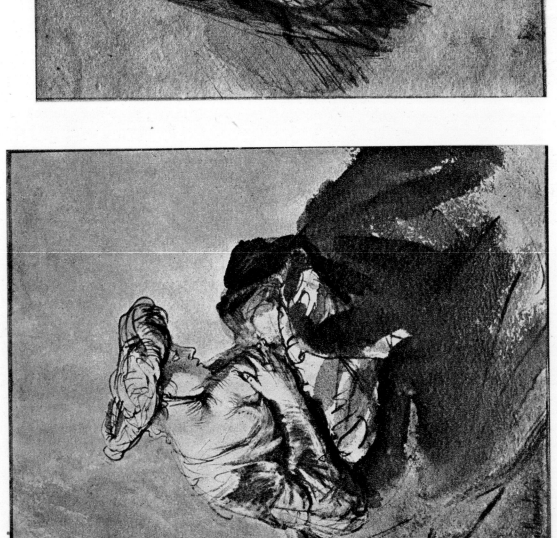

*95. WOMAN SUCKLING A CHILD. About 1636/37. Paris, Heirs of Henri Pereire.
(Pen and wash, 149 : 112)

*98. STUDIES OF A WOMAN READING AND AN ORIENTAL. Preparatory drawing for the etching B.37 of 1638, Joseph telling his Dreams. New York, S. Kramarsky. (Pen and wash, 139 : 125)

*97. ADAM AND EVE. Preparatory sketch for the etching B.28 of 1638. Amsterdam, Dr. A. Welcker. (Pen and wash, 115 : 115)

*99. PORTRAIT OF TITIA VAN UYLENBURCH. Dated 1639. Stockholm, Nationalmuseum.
(Pen and wash, 178 : 146)

*100. PORTRAIT OF BALDASSARE CASTIGLIONE AFTER RAPHAEL. Dated 1639. Vienna, Albertina. (Pen, 163 : 207)

*101. ARTIST DRAWING FROM A MODEL. Preparatory sketch for the etching B.192.
About 1639. London, British Museum. (Pen and wash, 185 : 160)

*102. PORTRAIT OF A LADY HOLDING A FAN. Preparatory drawing for the painting of 1639 in Amsterdam. London, British Museum. (Pen, red chalk, wash, 160 : 129)

R. Rosang.

*104. STUDY FOR THE GROUP OF THE SICK IN THE HUNDRED GUILDER PRINT. About 1639-40.
Berlin, Kupferstichkabinett.
(Pen and wash, 144 : 185)

*103. WOMAN AND CHILD. Study for the Hundred
Guilder Print. About 1638-40. Cambridge, Mass. U.S.,
Fogg Art Museum, Paul J. Sachs Collection. (Pen, 121 : 75)

*107. OLD MAN GUIDED BY A LITTLE BOY. About 1640.
Stockholm, Nationalmuseum.
(Pen and wash, 130 : 84)

*106. BLIND OLD MAN GUIDED BY A WOMAN. Study for the
Hundred Guilder Print. About 1639/40. Paris, Louvre.
(Pen, 122 : 98)

*105. MAN STANDING, A CAP IN HIS
OUTSTRETCHED RIGHT HAND. Study
for the Hundred Guilder Print. About 1639/40.
London, H. S. Reitlinger. (Pen, 127 : 58)

*108. NUDE MAN KNEELING. Study for the etching B.92 of 1640.
The Beheading of St. John the Baptist. Bayonne, Musée, Collection Bonnat.
(Pen, 99 : 91)

*109. BEHEADING OF PRISONERS. About 1640. Amsterdam, formerly Mensing Collection.
(Pen and wash, 175 : 125)

110. MANOAH'S OFFERING. About 1639. Berlin, Kupferstichkabinett. (Pen, 175 : 190)

*111. PORTRAIT OF CORNELIS CLAESZ ANSLO. Dated 1640. Preparatory drawing for the etching B.271 of 1641. London, British Museum. (Red chalk, 157 : 143)

112. VIEW OF LONDON WITH OLD ST. PAUL'S. About 1640. Berlin, Kupferstichkabinett. (Pen and wash, 164 : 318)

113. VIEW OVER A WIDE RIVER SCENERY WITH A WINDMILL. About 1640. Paris, Heirs of Henri Pereire. (Pen and wash, 205 : 325)

*114. COTTAGES BEFORE A STORMY SKY. About 1641. Vienna, Albertina. (Pen and wash, 182 : 245)

115. PASTURES WITH A WINDMILL OUTSIDE A TOWN. About 1641. Chantilly, Musée Condé. (Pen and wash, 142 : 288)

116. THE WINDMILL ON THE OUTERMOST BULWARK OF AMSTERDAM WITH THE VIEW OVER HET IJ. About 1641. Rotterdam, F. Koenigs Collection. (Black chalk, 166 : 275)

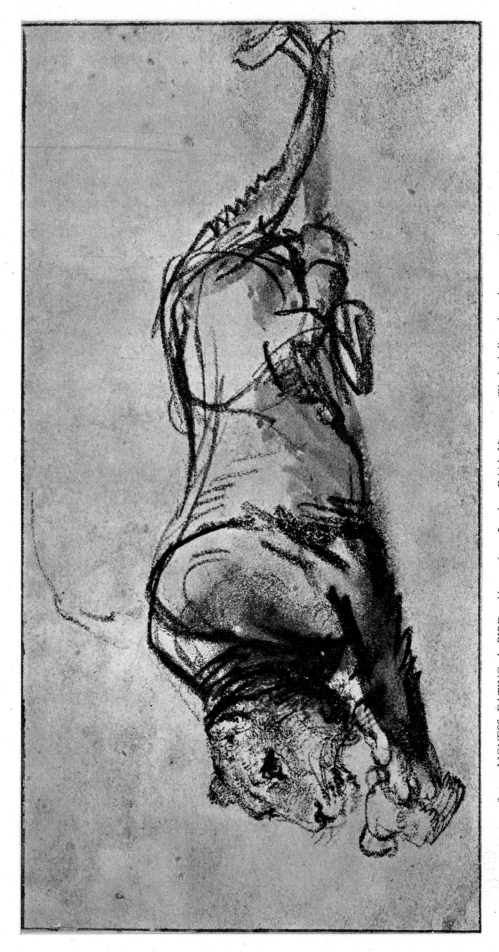

*117. LIONESS EATING A BIRD. About 1641. London, British Museum. (Black chalk and wash, 127 : 240)

*119. THE TRIUMPH OF MORDECAI. Preparatory drawing for the etching B.40. About 1640/41. Lwów, Lubomirski Museum. (Pen, 188 : 263)

*120. THE RAISING OF LAZARUS. About 1641/42. Rotterdam, Museum Boymans.
(Pen, 182 : 155)

*121. STUDIES OF AN OFFICER, AN ORIENTAL, AND A MAN IN HIGH CAP. Drawn in connection
with the Nightwatch (1642). Paris, Louvre, Walter Gay Bequest. (Pen, 212 : 134)

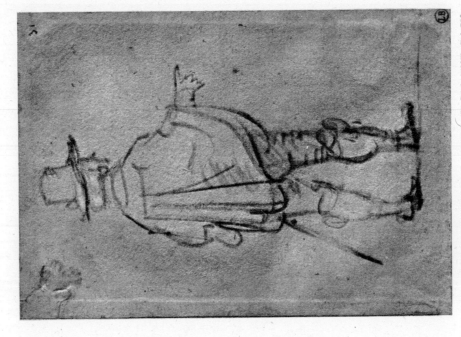

*123. OFFICER WALKING, SEEN FROM THE BACK.
Study made in connection with the Nightwatch (1642). Paris,
Louvre, Bonnat Bequest. (Black chalk, 122 : 83)

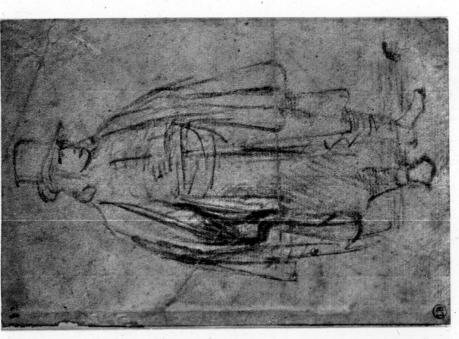

*122. YOUNG MAN IN STREET COSTUME, FULL-
LENGTH. About 1641/42. Paris, Louvre, Bonnat Bequest.
(Black chalk, 124 : 82)

*124. THE PRODIGAL SON WITH THE LOOSE WOMEN. About 1642/43. Basel, Robert von Hirsch. (Pen and wash, 177 : 210)

*126. TWO WOMEN WALKING. Study for the etching
B.120, Preciosa. About 1642. Brussels, Musée des Beaux-Arts,
Collection de Grez. (Black chalk, 129 : 82)

*125. THE SMOKER. Dated 1643.
Amsterdam, Dr. H. Tietje.
(Pen, 99 : 78)

*128. OLD WOMAN SEATED, HOLDING A BOOK AND EYE-GLASSES. Sketch connected with the painting of 1643 in Leningrad. Lwów, Lubomirski Museum. (Red chalk, 162 : 127)

*127. OLD WOMAN IN A LARGE HEAD-DRESS, HALF-LENGTH. Life study for the painting of 1643 in Leningrad. Dresden, Friedrich August II. (Black chalk, 140 : 110)

*129. THE BROTHERS OF JOSEPH REQUEST BENJAMIN FROM THEIR FATHER. About 1643. Amsterdam, Rijksprentenkabinet. (Pen, 176 : 231)

130. CHRIST PREACHING. Compositional sketch connected with the Hundred Guilder Print. About 1643. Paris, Louvre, Bonnat Bequest. (Pen, 198 : 230)

*131. VERTUMNUS AND POMONA. About 1643/44. Formerly J. Qu. van Regteren Altena, Amsterdam. (Pen and wash, 175 : 218)

132. TOBIAS FRIGHTENED BY THE FISH WITH THE ANGEL, IN A MOUNTAINOUS LANDSCAPE. About 1643/44. Berlin, Kupferstichkabinett.
(Pen and wash, 205 : 273)

133A. JAN PYNAS: LANDSCAPE WITH AN INN BESIDE A ROAD, AND A LITTLE PIG. Cracow, Czartoryski Museum.
(Pen and wash, 146 : 210)

133B. COPY BY REMBRANDT AFTER THE ABOVE DRAWING. About 1644. Rotterdam, F. Koenigs Collection
(Pen and wash, 141 : 202)

134. COTTAGE NEAR THE ENTRANCE OF A WOOD. Dated 1644. New York, Jacob Hirsch. (Pen and wash, 298 : 452)

*135. A CANAL BETWEEN BUSHES. Study after nature, used in the etching B.231 of 1645.
The Boat-House. Lwów, Lubomirski Museum. (Black chalk, 155 : 117)

*136. ESAU SELLING HIS BIRTHRIGHT. About 1645. Amsterdam, Museum Fodor.
(Pen, 155 : 148)

*137. THE HOLY FAMILY IN THE CARPENTER'S WORKSHOP. Preparatory drawing for the painting of 1645 in
Leningrad. Bayonne, Musée, Collection Bonnat. (Pen, 161 : 158)

*138. BABY SLEEPING IN A CRADLE. Life study, probably connected with
the painting in Leningrad. About 1645. Heirs of Sir Henry Oppenheimer, London.
(Black chalk, 75 : 113)

139. THE HOLY FAMILY ASLEEP, WITH ANGELS. About 1645. Cambridge, Louis C. G. Clarke.
(Pen, 175 : 213)

*140. TOBIT AND ANNA WITH THE GOAT. Sketch connected with the painting of 1645 in Berlin. Berlin, Kupferstichkabinett. (Pen, 146 : 185)

*141. ABRAHAM ENTERTAINING THE ANGELS. Preparatory drawing for the painting of 1646 in Heemstede, Mrs. C. von Pannwitz. New York, K Riezler. (Pen and wash, 106 : 128)

*142. BUST OF A GIRL. About 1645.
Brussels, Musée des Beaux-Arts, Collection de Grez. (Black chalk, 73 : 52)

*143. YOUNG GIRL LEANING OUT OF A
WINDOW. Life Study for the painting of 1645
in Dulwich College. Dresden, Friedrich August II.
(Black chalk, 83 : 65)

*144. MAN LOOKING OUT OF A WINDOW, HOLDING
HIS CAP. About 1646. Paris, Petit Palais, Collection Dutuit.
(Pen, 101 : 76)

*145. THE PREACHER JAN CORNELISZ SYLVIUS. About 1645.
Dresden, Friedrich August II. (Pen, 133 : 122)

146. PORTRAIT OF JAN CORNELISZ SYLVIUS. Preparatory drawing for the etching B.280 of 1646. London, British Museum.
(Pen and wash, 283 : 193)

*147. JAN SIX WITH A DOG, STANDING BY AN OPEN WINDOW.
Preparatory drawing for the etching B.285 of 1647. Amsterdam, Six Collection. (Pen and wash, 220 : 175)

*148. MALE NUDE STANDING. Life study for the etching B.194. About 1646. London, British Museum.
(Pen, wash, red and black chalk, 252 : 193)

*149. FEMALE NUDE LYING ON CUSHIONS. About 1646. Hamburg, Kunsthalle. (Black chalk, 165 : 265)

150. THE SINGEL IN AMERSFOORT. About 1647/48. Paris, Louvre. (Pen and wash, 153 : 277)

151. VIEW OF RHENEN. About 1647/48. The Hague, Bredius Museum. (Pen and wash, 210 : 324)

*152. THE WESTERPOORT AT RHENEN. About 1647/48. Haarlem, Museum Teyler. (Pen and wash, 165 : 226)

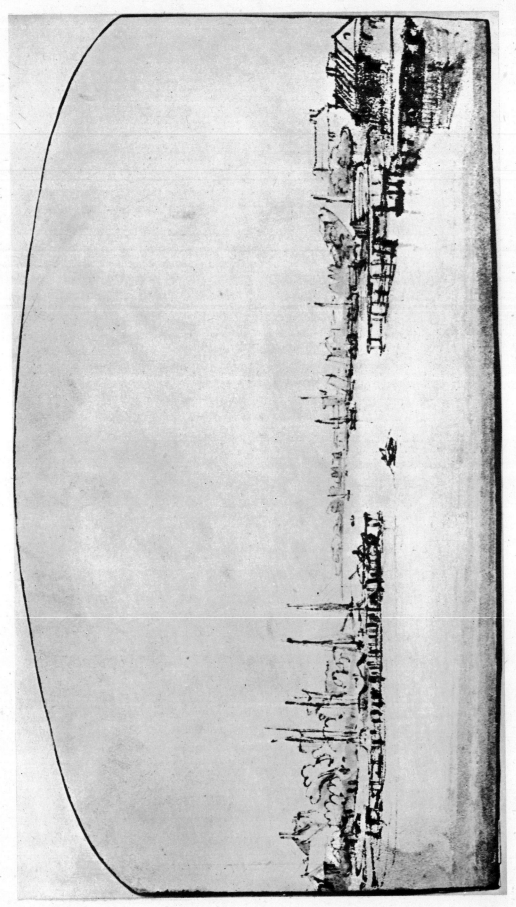

*153. VIEW OVER THE AMSTEL. About 1648/50. Amsterdam, Rijksprentenkabinet. (Pen and wash, 132 : 232)

154. THE BEND OF THE AMSTEL RIVER, NEAR KOSTVERLOREN. About 1648/50. Paris, Louvre, E. de Rothschild Bequest. (Pen and wash, 148 : 269)

155. LITTLE BRIDGE CROSSING A CANAL BETWEEN TREES. About 1648/50. Haarlem, Museum Teyler. (Pen and wash, 190 : 270)

*156. WOODY LANDSCAPE WITH A HORSEMAN. About 1648/50. Leningrad, Hermitage. (Pen and wash, 157 : 234)

157. THE PRESENTATION IN THE TEMPLE. About 1647. Paris, Louvre, E. de Rothschild Bequest.
(Pen and wash, 238 : 208)

*158. THE CALVARY. About 1647. Frankfort-on-Main, Städelsches Kunstinstitut. (Pen and wash, 165 : 238)

*159. ESAU SELLING HIS BIRTHRIGHT TO JACOB. About 1648/49. London, British Museum.
(Pen and wash, 200 : 173)

160. THE GOOD SAMARITAN DISMOUNTING THE WOUNDED FROM THE MULE.   About 1648.   Weimar, Grossherzogliches Museum.
(Pen, 197 : 205)

161. THE GOOD SAMARITAN ARRIVING AT THE INN. About 1648. London, British Museum. (Pen and wash, 184 : 286)

162. POTIPHAR'S WIFE ACCUSING JOSEPH. About 1648/49. London, Dr. Delbanco. (Pen and wash, 201 : 267)

*163. ST. PETER AND ST. JOHN HEALING THE PARALYSED AT THE GATE OF THE TEMPLE. About 1648/49.
New York, Courtesy of the Metropolitan Museum of Art. (Pen and wash, 205 : 162)

*164. CHRIST AND THE WOMAN OF SAMARIA. About 1648/49. Birmingham, Barber Institute.
(Pen, 207 : 187)

*165. THE PARABLE OF THE UNWORTHY WEDDING GUEST. About 1648/49. Vienna, Albertina. (Pen and wash, 183 : 265)

*166. HARVESTERS IN A FIELD RESTING. About 1649/50. Paris, Atherton Curtis. (Pen, 176 : 250)

167. CHRIST ON THE CROSS. About 1649/50. Paris, Atherton Curtis. (Pen, 270 : 198)

168. OLD MAN SEATED IN AN ARM-CHAIR. About 1650.
City of Danzig Museum. (Black chalk, 130 : 93)

*169. SEATED OLD MAN WITH A STICK. On the reverse, the date 1650.
Dresden, Kupferstichkabinett. (Pen, 130 : 110)

170. FARM-BUILDINGS BESIDE A ROAD. Study after nature for the etching B.213, The Landscape with the Milkman. About 1650. Oxford, Ashmolean Museum. (Pen and wash, 113 : 247)

*171. FARM-HOUSE AMONG TREES BESIDE A CANAL WITH A ROWING-BOAT. About 1650. Chatsworth, The Duke of Devonshire. (Pen and wash, 133 : 200)

172. FARM-HOUSE BENEATH TREES AND A FOOT-BRIDGE. Study, used for the
etching B.222 of 1652. Cambridge, Fitzwilliam Museum. (Pen and wash, 157 : 181)

173. THE RUINS OF THE OLD CITY HALL IN AMSTERDAM AFTER THE FIRE. Dated 1652. Amsterdam, Rembrandt-huis.
(Pen and wash, 150 : 201)

174. A COTTAGE AMONG TREES. About 1650. New York, Courtesy of the Metropolitan Museum of Art. (Pen and wash, 172 : 275)

*175.   ROAD IN A WOOD LEADING INTO THE DISTANCE.   About 1650.   Chatsworth, The Duke of Devonshire.
(Pen and wash, 156 : 200)

*176. A THATCHED COTTAGE BY A TREE. About 1650/51. Chatsworth, The Duke of Devonshire. (Pen, 175 : 267)

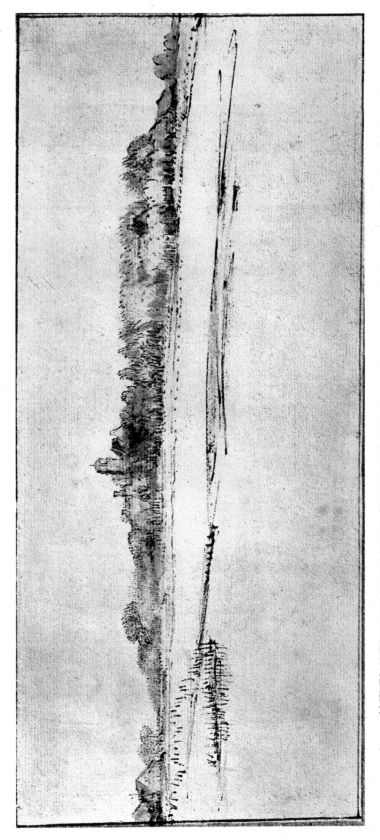

*177. AMSTEL VIEW WITH THE CASTLE KOSTVERLOREN. About 1651. London, O. Gutekunst. (Pen and wash, 98 : 216)

*178. THE AMSTEL RIVER WITH TWO SAILING-BOATS. About 1651.
Paris, Ecole des Beaux-Arts. (Black chalk, 92 : 150)

*179. OPEN LANDSCAPE WITH HAARLEM IN THE DISTANCE. Study after nature, used in the etching
B.234 of 1651, The Goldweigher's Field. Rotterdam, F. Koenigs Collection. (Pen and wash, 89 : 152)

*180. A WINTER LANDSCAPE. About 1649/50. Cambridge, Massachusetts, Fogg Museum of Art.
(Pen and wash, 67 : 161)

*181. VIEW OF HOUTEWAAL. About 1651. Chatsworth, The Duke of Devonshire. (Pen and wash, 125 : 182)

182. ST. JEROME READING, IN AN ITALIAN LANDSCAPE. Preparatory drawing for the etching B.104. About 1652. Hamburg, Kunsthalle.
(Pen and wash, 250 : 207)

*183. LION RESTING. About 1652. Spiez, J. de Bruijn. (Pen and brush, 140 : 205)

*184. THE ANGEL APPEARING TO JOSEPH IN HIS DREAM. About 1651/52. Sketch used for the painting in Budapest.
Berlin, Kupferstichkabinett. (Pen and wash, 145 : 187)

*185. CHRIST DISPUTING WITH THE DOCTORS. About 1652. Paris, Louvre, Bonnat Bequest. (Pen, 189 : 259)

186. CHRIST AND NICODEMUS. About 1652. Vienna, Albertina. (Pen and wash, 200 : 271)

*187. THE HOLY FAMILY. About 1652. Vienna, Albertina. (Pen and wash, 220 : 191)

*188. THE ANNUNCIATION. Drawing by a pupil, corrected by Rembrandt. About 1652. Berlin, Kupferstichkabinett. (Red chalk, pen and wash, 173 : 231)

*189. THE ANGEL LEAVES THE FAMILY OF TOBIT. About 1652. New York, Courtesy of the Pierpont Morgan Library. (Pen, 193 : 243)

*190. THE FORTUNE-TELLER. About 1652. Geneva, Musée d'Art et d'Histoire.
(Pen, 99 : 122)

*191. ISAAC BLESSING JACOB. About 1652. London, Lady Melchett. (Pen, 120 : 125)

*192. THE ANGEL APPEARING TO JOSEPH IN HIS DREAM. About 1652. Amsterdam, Rijksprentenkabinet, Hofstede de Groot Bequest.
(Pen, 179 : 181)

*193. THE VISION OF DANIEL. Preparatory drawing for the painting in Berlin. About 1652. Paris, Louvre, Bonnat Bequest. (Pen and wash, 165 : 242)

*194. TOBIAS AND THE ANGEL AT THE RIVER. About 1652. Paris, Louvre, Bonnat Bequest. (Pen 179 : 263)

*195. HOMER RECITING VERSES. Dated 1652. Drawing in the Pandora Album of the Six Family. Amsterdam, Six Collection.
(Pen, 255 : 180)

*196. JAN SIX'S MOTHER AS PALLAS IN HER STUDY. Dated 1652. Drawing in the Pandora Album
of the Six Family. Amsterdam, Six Collection. (Pen and wash, 190 : 140)

197. CHRIST CARRYING THE CROSS. About 1653. Haarlem, Museum Teyler. (Pen and wash, 174 : 272)

198. CHRIST ON THE CROSS. About 1653. Stockholm, Nationalmuseum. (Pen and wash, 250 : 218)

199. CHRIST FINDING THE APOSTLES ASLEEP IN THE GARDEN GETHSEMANE. About 1654. Formerly J. P. Heseltine, London. (Pen and wash, 185 : 280)

200. CHRIST IN THE STORM ON THE SEA OF GALILEE. About 1654/55. Dresden, Kupferstichkabinett. (Pen, 197 : 300)

*201. QUINTUS FABIUS MAXIMUS. Sketch for the
painting of 1655 in Belgrade. Berlin, Kupferstichkabinett.
(Pen, 111 : 74)

*202. CHRIST AND THE WOMAN OF SAMARIA. About 1655. Oxford, Ashmolean Museum.
(Pen, 96 : 142)

*203. YOUNG WOMAN READING. About 1655.
Stockholm, Nationalmuseum. (Pen and wash, 109 : 90)

*204. THE SLAUGHTERED OX. About 1655. Berlin Kupferstichkabinett. (Pen and wash, 134 : 179)

*205. ST. JOHN THE BAPTIST PREACHING. About 1655. Paris, Louvre, Bonnat Bequest. (Pen and wash, 145 : 204)

*206. WOMEN SEWING IN REMBRANDT'S HOUSE. About 1654/55. Amsterdam, Dr. N. Beets. (Pen and wash, 135 : 200)

*207, MOSES BEFORE THE BURNING BUSH. About 1654/55. London, Sir Herbert Bonn. (Pen and wash, 175 : 242)

209. ST. PETER'S PRAYER BEFORE THE RAISING OF TABITHA. About 1654/55. Bayonne, Musée, Collection Bonnat.
(Pen and wash, 190 : 200)

*210. THE PROPHET JONAH BEFORE THE WALLS OF NINIVEH. About 1654/55. Vienna, Albertina.
(Pen and wash, 217 : 173)

L'ange quitte Manüé et Sa femme, et s'éleve au milieu de la flame qu'il avoit exciteé 1807. 79

211. MANOAH'S OFFERING. About 1655. Stockholm, Nationalmuseum. (Pen and wash, 233 : 203)

270

212. MANOAH'S OFFERING. Project for the alteration of the painting of 1641 in Dresden. About 1655. Winterthur, Dr. O. Reinhart. (Pen and wash, 190 : 280)

*213. THE CHURCH OF RANSDORP IN WATERLAND.
About 1652/53. Oxford, Ashmolean Museum.
(Pen and wash, 131 : 89)

*214. FARM-HOUSE AND TREES WITH A CANAL IN THE FOREGROUND. About 1652/53. Stockholm, Nationalmuseum.
(Pen and wash, 108 : 175)

*215. THE MONTELBAANSTOREN IN AMSTERDAM. About 1652/53. Amsterdam, Rembrandt-huis.
(Pen and wash, 145 : 144)

*216. THATCHED COTTAGE BY A TREE. About 1653. Vienna, Akademie der Bildenden Künste.
(Pen and wash, 90 : 138)

*217. COTTAGE WITH A HAY-BARN AND WEIRS BESIDE A STREAM. About 1652/53. Chatsworth, The Duke of Devonshire.
(Pen and wash, 116 : 202)

*219. THE RIJNPOORT AT RHENEN. About 1652/53. Paris, Louvre. (Pen and wash, 146 : 252)

*220.   WINDMILLS ON THE WEST SIDE OF AMSTERDAM.   About 1653.   Copenhagen, Dr. G. Falck.   (Pen and wash, 120 : 263)

*222. COTTAGE AND TREES BY A STREAM. About 1653. New York, Copyright The Frick Collection. (Pen and wash, 156 : 226)

*223. WINDMILL ON A BULWARK OF AMSTERDAM. About 1653/54. F. Lugt Collection. (Pen and wash, 114 : 202)

*224. LARGE TREE BY A DIKE WITH A CART PASSING BY. About 1653/54. Paris, Louvre, Walter Gay Bequest. (Pen and wash, 150 : 231)

*225. THE ANGLER. About 1654/55. Stockholm, Nationalmuseum. (Pen, 126 : 172)

*226. CANAL WITH A BRIDGE BESIDE A TALL TREE. About 1654/55. New York, Courtesy of the Pierpont Morgan Library. (Pen and wash, 140 : 243)

*227. VIEW OF THE AMSTEL WITH A MAN BATHING. About 1654/55. Berlin, Kupferstichkabinett. (Pen and wash, 146 : 273)

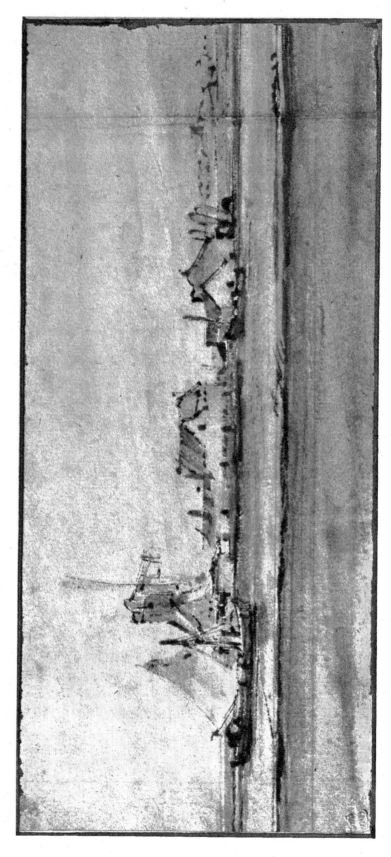

*228. "HET MOLENTJE", SEEN FROM THE AMSTELDIJK. About 1654/55. Vienna, Albertina. (Pen and wash, 96 : 213)

*229. SHAH JAHAN, Copy after an Indian Miniature. About 1654/56. Basel, Robert von Hirsch.
(Pen and wash, 225 : 171)

*230. AN ORIENTAL CAVALIER. Copy after an Indian Miniature. About 1654/56. London, British Museum.
(Pen and wash, red chalk, yellow water colour, 206 : 177)

*231. FOUR ORIENTALS SEATED BENEATH A TREE. Copy after an Indian Miniature, used for the etching B.29 of 1656, Abraham entertaining the Angels. London, British Museum. (Pen and wash, 194 : 125)

*232. TIMOUR ENTHRONED. Copy after an Indian Miniature. About 1654/56. Paris, Louvre.
(Pen and wash, 186 : 187)

*233. MANOAH'S OFFERING. About 1655/56. New York, Schaeffer Galleries. (Pen, 205 : 177)

*234. THE PRESENTATION IN THE TEMPLE. About 1655/56. Paris, Atherton Curtis.
(Pen, 160 : 139)

*235. JOSEPH BEFORE PHARAOH. About 1655/56. Berlin, Kupferstichkabinett. (Pen, 189 : 179)

*236. JACOB IS SHOWN THE BLOOD-STAINED COAT OF JOSEPH. About 1655/56. Rotterdam, F. Koenigs Collection.
(Pen, 133 : 179)

*237. THE RETURN OF THE PRODIGAL SON. About 1655/56. F. Lugt Collection.
(Pen, 165 : 120)

*238. GIRL ASLEEP, RESTING ON A CUSHION. About 1656.
Amsterdam, Rembrandt-huis. (Pen and wash, 139 : 99)

*239. STUDY OF A SICK WOMAN IN BED AND A NURSE. About 1656. London, O. Gutekunst.
(Pen and wash, 101 : 169)

*240. CHRIST AND THE TWO DISCIPLES ON THEIR WAY TO EMMAUS. About 1655/56. Paris, Louvre. (Pen, 166 : 224)

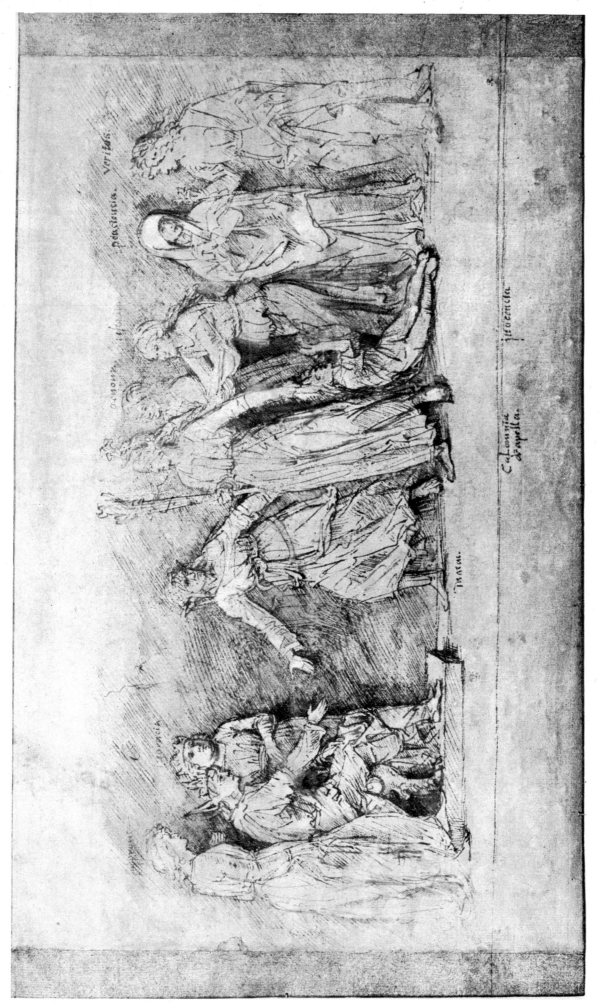

241. THE CALUMNY OF APELLES. Copy after a drawing of the School of Mantegna. About 1656. London, British Museum. (Pen and wash, 263 : 394)

*242. FEMALE NUDE SEATED ON A CHAIR, SEEN FROM BEHIND. About 1655/56. Munich, Graphische Sammlung.
(Pen and brush, 222 : 185)

243. FEMALE NUDE SEATED BEFORE A STOVE. About 1655/56. Rotterdam, F. Koenigs Collection.
(Pen and brush, 272 : 195)

*244. REMBRANDT'S STUDIO. About 1655/56. Oxford, Ashmolean Museum. (Pen and brush, 205 : 190)

*245.   WOMAN LOOKING OUT OF A WINDOW.   About 1655/56.   Paris, Louvre, E. de Rothschild Bequest.
(Pen and brush, 292 : 162)

*246. JAN SIX WRITING AT HIS ESTATE IJMOND (?). About 1655/56. Paris, Louvre.
(Pen and wash, 135 : 197)

*247. BOY DRAWING AT A DESK (PROBABLY TITUS). About 1655/56. Dresden, Kupferstichkabinett.
(Pen and brush, 182 : 140)

*248. GIRL LEANING IN A WINDOW, ASLEEP. About 1655/56. Stockholm, Nationalmuseum.
(Pen and wash, 162 : 174)

249. GIRL SLEEPING. About 1655/56. London, British Museum. (Brush, 245 : 203)

*250. SELF-PORTRAIT, FULL-LENGTH. About 1655/56. Amsterdam, Rembrandt-huis.
(Pen, 203 : 134)

*251. BOY IN A WIDE-BRIMMED HAT, RESTING HIS CHIN
ON HIS HAND. About 1655/56. London, British Museum.(Pen, 85 : 90)

*252. THE ANATOMY LESSON OF DR. JOAN DEIJMAN. Sketch for the painting of 1656
in Amsterdam. Amsterdam, Rijksprentenkabinet. (Pen, 110 : 133)

253. GOD ANNOUNCES HIS COVENANT TO ABRAHAM. About 1656. Dresden, Kupferstichkabinett. (Pen, 197 : 266)

254. THE DISMISSAL OF HAGAR. About 1656. New York, Courtesy of The Pierpont Morgan Library. (Pen, 206 : 213)

*255. THE SEIZURE OF CHRIST. About 1656/57. Dresden, Friedrich August II. (Pen and wash, 175 : 260)

256. THE ANNUNCIATION TO THE SHEPHERDS. About 1656/57. Amsterdam, Rijksprentenkabinet, Hofstede de Groot Bequest. (Pen and wash, 188 : 280)

*257. CHRIST HEALING A LEPER. About 1656/57. Amsterdam, Rijksprentenkabinet, Hofstede de Groot Bequest. (Pen, 147 : 172)

*258. THE MOCKING OF CHRIST. About 1656/57. Bayonne, Musée, Collection Bonnat. (Pen, 181 : 245)

*259. THE PROPHET ELISHA AND THE WIDOW WITH HER SONS. About 1657. Vienna, The Prince of Liechtenstein. (Pen, 172 : 254)

*260. SAUL AND HIS SERVANTS WITH THE WITCH OF ENDOR. About 1657. The Hague, Bredius Museum. (Pen and wash, 144 : 226)

261. COTTAGES BENEATH HIGH TREES IN BRIGHT SUNLIGHT. About 1657/58. Berlin, Kupferstichkabinett. (Pen and wash, 195 : 310)

262. FEMALE NUDE WITH HER HEAD BENT FORWARD, ASLEEP. About 1657/58. Amsterdam, Rijksprentenkabinet. (Pen and brush, 142 : 284)

*263. THE PRESENTATION IN THE TEMPLE. Preparatory drawing for the etching B.50. About 1657/58. Rotterdam, F. Koenigs Collection. (Pen, 162 : 118)

264. THE RAISING OF THE CROSS. About 1657/58. Berlin, Kupferstichkabinett.
(Pen and wash, 179 : 211)

265. THE ENTOMBMENT OF CHRIST. Copy after a drawing of the School of Raphael. About 1657/58. Haarlem, Museum Teyler. (Pen and wash, 180 : 283)

*266. CHRIST AND THE WOMAN TAKEN IN ADULTERY. About 1658/59. Stockholm, Nationalmuseum. (Pen, 189 : 248)

*267. REMBRANDT HIMSELF, DRAWING.
About 1657/58. Rotterdam, F. Koenigs
Collection. (Pen, 69 : 62)

*268. WOMAN SUCKLING A CHILD. About 1657/58. Formerly Rathenau
Collection, Berlin. (Pen, 142 : 113)

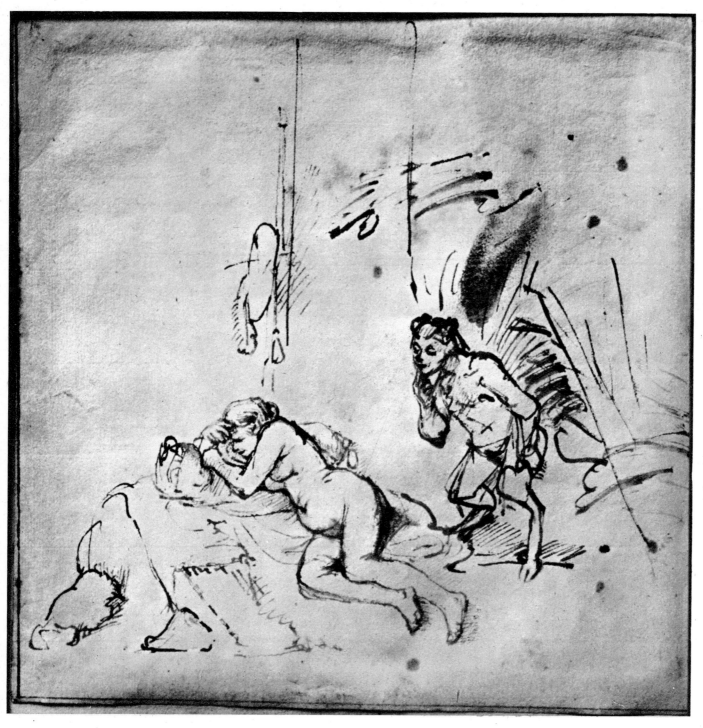

*269. JUPITER AND ANTIOPE. About 1658/59. Paris, Louvre, Walter Gay Bequest. (Pen, 188 : 188)

*270. JAEL AND SISERA. About 1659/60. Amsterdam, Rijksprentenkabinet, Hofstede de Groot Bequest.
(Pen, 190 : 172)

*271. CHRIST HEALING A SICK WOMAN. About 1659/60. Formerly W. Bode Collection, Berlin.
(Pen. 172 : 188)

272. CHRIST WALKING ON THE WAVES. About 1659/60. London, British Museum. (Pen, 191 : 290)

273. THE SEIZURE OF CHRIST. About 1659/60. Stockholm, Nationalmuseum. (Pen and wash, 205 : 298)

*274. CHRIST AND THE WOMAN TAKEN IN ADULTERY. About 1659/60. Cologne, Wallraf-Richartz Museum.
(Pen, 100 : 166)

*275. THE DENIAL OF ST. PETER. Sketch for the painting of 1660 in Amsterdam.
Madrid, Biblioteca Nacional. (Pen, 84 : 110)

*276. THE PRESENTATION IN THE TEMPLE. Drawing in
the Album of Jacobus Heyblock, dated 1661. The Hague,
Royal Library. (Pen and brush, 120 : 89)

*277. OLD MAN READING, IN PROFILE TO THE LEFT.
About 1661. Stockholm, Nationalmuseum, (Pen, 104 : 95)

59

278. FEMALE NUDE SURROUNDED BY A DRAPERY. Preparatory drawing for the etching of 1661,
The Woman with the Arrow, B.202. London, British Museum. (Pen and brush, 298 : 193)

*279. THE CONSPIRACY OF JULIUS CIVILIS. Preparatory drawing for the painting in the City Hall of Amsterdam. About 1660/61.
Munich, Graphische Sammlung. (Pen and wash, 196 : 180)

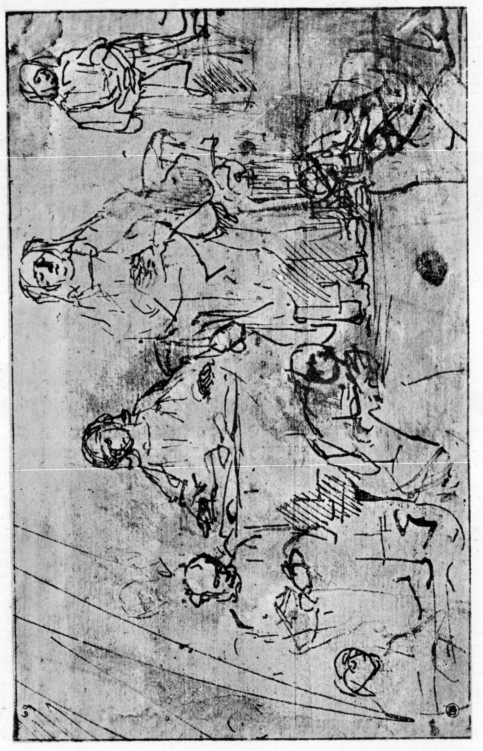

*280. STUDY FOR A RELIGIOUS SCENE (PENTECOST ?) About 1660/61. Paris, Louvre, Bonnat Bequest. (Pen, 125 : 194)

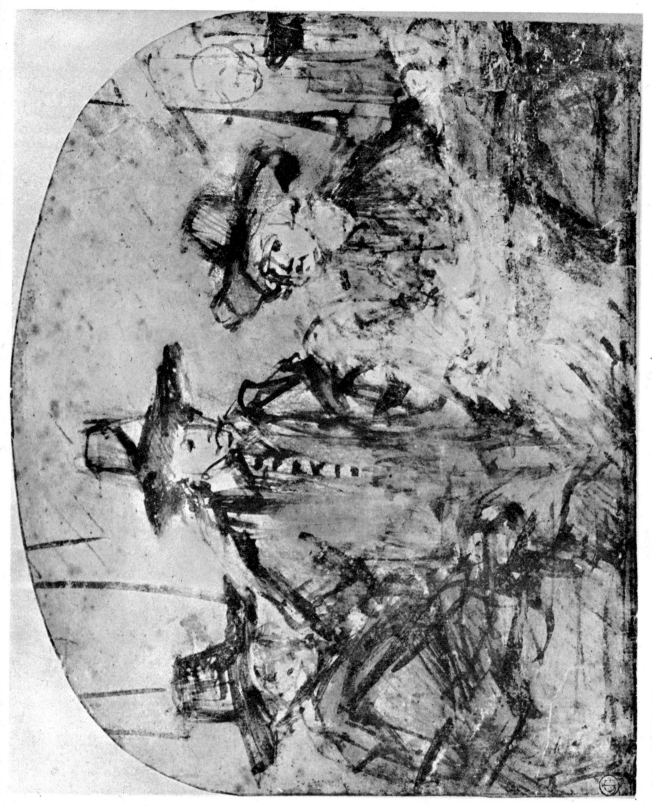

*282 THE STANDING STAALMEESTER. Life Study for the painting of 1662 in Amsterdam. Rotterdam, F. Koenigs Collection.
(Pen and wash, 225 : 175)

283. PORTRAIT OF A YOUNG MAN (TITUS ?), THREE-QUARTER-LENGTH. About 1662. Amsterdam, Six Collection.
(Pen, 232 : 194)

*284. A CHILD BEING TAUGHT TO WALK. About 1660/62. London, British Museum.
(Pen, 93 : 156)

285. DIFFERENT STUDIES FOR A LIBERATION OF ST. PETER AND OTHER SUBJECTS. About 1660/62. Dresden, Kupferstichkabinett. (Pen, 195 : 265).

*286. A LION LYING DOWN. About 1660/62. Amsterdam, Rijksprentenkabinet. (Pen, 119 : 212)

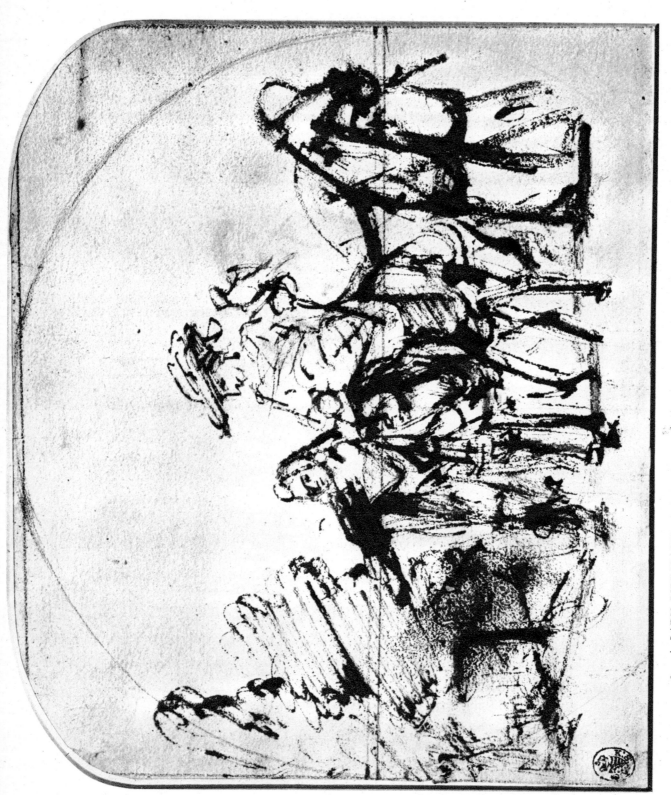

287. A LADY RIDING OUT, HAWKING. About 1662/65. Dresden, Kupferstichkabinett. (Pen, 214 : 252)

288. ST. PETER AT THE DEATH-BED OF TABITHA. About 1662/65. Dresden, Kupferstichkabinett. (Pen, 190 : 273.)

289. DIANA AND ACTAEON. Drawing after an engraving by A. Tempesta. About 1662/65. Dresden, Kupferstichkabinett. (Pen and wash, 246 : 347)

*290. PORTRAIT STUDIES OF TWO WOMEN, HALF-LENGTHS. About 1665/69. Dresden, Kupferstichkabinett.
(Pen, 137 : 183)

*291.   YOUNG MAN HOLDING A FLOWER, THREE-QUARTER-LENGTH.
About 1665/69. Paris, Louvre. (Pen and wash, 175 : 118)

*292. SELF-PORTRAIT. Study for the painting of
1660 in the Louvre. Vienna, Albertina.
(Pen and wash, 84 : 71)

LIST OF PLATES

PRINTED IN
GREAT BRITAIN
BY CLARKE & SHERWELL
NORTHAMPTON